KRISHNA MOHAN AVANCHA

Leadership or Kingship!!

Copyright © 2023 by Krishna Mohan Avancha

All rights reserved. No part of this publication may be reproduced, stored or transmitted in any form or by any means, electronic, mechanical, photocopying, recording, scanning, or otherwise without written permission from the publisher. It is illegal to copy this book, post it to a website, or distribute it by any other means without permission.

First edition

This book was professionally typeset on Reedsy. Find out more at reedsy.com

Contents

1 The Foundations of Leadership: Defining Leadership,... 1
2 Understanding Leadership Styles: Autocratic, Democratic,... 8
3 The Qualities of a Leader: Character, Vision, Communication,... 10
4 Developing Leadership Skills: Emotional Intelligence,... 12
5 Leading Teams: Building Trust, Motivating, and Delegating... 18
6 Managing Conflict: Strategies for Resolving Disputes and... 22
7 Building a Culture of Accountability: Setting Expectations,... 27
8 Leading Change: Planning and Implementing Organizational... 31
9 Ethics and Values: Balancing Personal and Organizational... 36
10 Leadership in a Global World: Cross-cultural Communication... 43
11 The Foundations of Kingship: History and Evolution of... 45
12 The Role of the King: Power, Responsibilities, and... 47
13 The Qualities of a King: Wisdom, Justice, and Courage 49
14 The King's Advisors: Choosing the Right People, and... 55
15 Maintaining the Stability of the Kingdom: Economic Policies,... 59
16 Diplomacy and Warfare: Building Alliances and Preparing for... 62
17 The King's Relationship with Religion and Culture: Balancing... 68
18 The King's Legacy: Building Monuments, Writing History, and... 72
19 Kingship in the Modern World: Evolving Concepts of Kingship... 75
20 Lessons from Great Kings: Case Studies of Successful Kings... 78

1

The Foundations of Leadership: Defining Leadership, Historical Examples, and Theories

Leadership is the art of inspiring, influencing, and directing individuals or groups towards a common goal or objective. It is a fundamental aspect of human society, and its impact can be seen in every aspect of our lives. In this article, we will discuss the foundations of leadership, including defining leadership, historical examples, and theories of leadership.

Defining Leadership:

Leadership is a complex and multifaceted concept that can be defined in many different ways. Some of the most common definitions of leadership include:

- Leadership is the ability to influence and inspire others to achieve a common goal.
- Leadership is the process of directing and coordinating the efforts of a group of individuals towards a shared objective.
- Leadership is the art of motivating people to act towards a desired outcome.

Historical Examples:

Throughout history, there have been many examples of great leaders who have made a significant impact on the world. Some of the most well-known historical leaders include:

- Alexander the Great: Alexander the Great was a military genius who conquered much of the known world during his reign. He was known for his strategic thinking and his ability to inspire his soldiers to fight with courage and determination.
- Mahatma Gandhi: Gandhi was a political and spiritual leader who led the Indian independence movement against British colonial rule. He is best known for his philosophy of nonviolent resistance and his commitment to social justice.
- Martin Luther King Jr.: King was an American civil rights leader who advocated for racial equality and social justice. He is best known for his speeches and his leadership in the Montgomery bus boycott and the March on Washington.

Theories of Leadership:

There are many different theories of leadership, each of which offers a unique perspective on the nature of leadership and the qualities that make a good leader. Some of the most well-known leadership theories include:

- Trait Theory: Trait theory suggests that certain innate characteristics, such as intelligence, charisma, and confidence, are essential for effective leadership.

Trait theory is a leadership theory that suggests that certain innate characteristics or traits are essential for effective leadership. This theory assumes that people are born with certain inherent traits that predispose them to become leaders.

According to trait theory, some of the most important leadership traits include:

1. Intelligence: Effective leaders must be intelligent, as they need to be able to understand complex problems and make informed decisions.
2. Confidence: Leaders must be self-assured and confident in their abilities, as this inspires confidence in their followers.
3. Charisma: Leaders must have a certain charisma or charm that attracts and motivates people to follow them.
4. Emotional stability: Leaders must be emotionally stable and able to handle stress and pressure, as they are often faced with difficult decisions and situations.
5. Openness to experience: Leaders must be open-minded and willing to try new things, as this allows them to adapt to changing circumstances and make innovative decisions.

Trait theory has been the subject of much debate and criticism over the years. Some critics argue that the theory oversimplifies the complex nature of leadership by suggesting that leadership can be reduced to a set of fixed traits. Others argue that the theory ignores the role of situational factors, such as the environment, culture, and context, in shaping leadership effectiveness.

Despite its limitations, trait theory has had a significant impact on the study of leadership and has influenced the development of other leadership theories. Many researchers continue to explore the relationship between leadership traits and effectiveness, and some have proposed more nuanced approaches to trait theory that take into account the role of situational factors.

One of the key contributions of trait theory is its emphasis on the importance of self-awareness and self-assessment in leadership development. By understanding their own strengths and weaknesses, leaders can develop a more comprehensive understanding of their leadership style and identify areas for improvement.

- Situational Theory: Situational theory suggests that the effectiveness of a leader depends on the situation they are in and their ability to adapt their leadership style to suit the needs of the situation.

Situational theory is a leadership theory that suggests that the effectiveness of a leader depends on the situation they are in. This theory proposes that there is no one-size-fits-all approach to leadership, and that different situations require different leadership styles.

According to situational theory, effective leaders are those who are able to adapt their leadership style to fit the needs of their followers and the demands of the situation. This theory identifies two key components of leadership effectiveness: leadership style and situational favorability.

Leadership style refers to the way in which a leader interacts with their followers. Situational theory proposes that there are two primary leadership styles: directive and supportive. Directive leaders provide clear guidance and structure to their followers, while supportive leaders focus on creating a positive and supportive environment.

Situational favorability refers to the degree to which a situation is favorable to the leader. Situational theory proposes that situational favorability depends on three key factors: task structure, leader-member relations, and leader position power. Task structure refers to the degree to which tasks are clearly defined and structured. Leader-member relations refer to the quality of the relationship between the leader and their followers. Leader position power refers to the amount of formal authority the leader has over their followers.

Situational theory suggests that there are four different leadership styles that can be used depending on the level of situational favorability. These leadership styles are:

1. Directing: This leadership style is appropriate when the task is highly structured, and the leader has a high level of position power but poor leader-member relations.
2. Coaching: This leadership style is appropriate when the task is moderately structured, and the leader has a high level of position power and good leader-member relations.
3. Supporting: This leadership style is appropriate when the task is unstructured, and the leader has a low level of position power but good leader-member relations.

4. Delegating: This leadership style is appropriate when the task is highly structured, and the leader has a low level of position power but good leader-member relations.

Situational theory has been widely researched and has been shown to be an effective approach to leadership in many different contexts. Studies have found that leaders who are able to adapt their leadership style to fit the demands of the situation are more effective than those who use a one-size-fits-all approach.

Despite its strengths, situational theory has been criticized for its lack of specificity and for its emphasis on the leader's role in adapting to the situation. Critics have argued that the theory does not adequately address the role of followers or the role of situational factors in shaping leadership effectiveness.

In response to these criticisms, some researchers have proposed more nuanced approaches to situational theory that take into account the role of followers and the complex interactions between leaders and followers.

- Transformational Theory: Transformational theory suggests that effective leaders inspire and motivate their followers to achieve a common goal by creating a vision and providing support and encouragement.

Transformational theory is a leadership theory that suggests that effective leaders inspire and motivate their followers to achieve a common goal by creating a vision and providing support and encouragement. According to this theory, leaders who are transformational have the ability to inspire their followers to exceed their own expectations and to work towards a higher purpose or goal.

Transformational leaders are characterized by several key traits:

1. Vision: Transformational leaders have a clear and compelling vision of the future that they communicate to their followers.
2. Charisma: Transformational leaders have a certain charisma or charm that inspires and motivates their followers.

3. Inspiration: Transformational leaders inspire their followers to exceed their own expectations and to work towards a higher purpose or goal.
4. Intellectual stimulation: Transformational leaders encourage their followers to think critically and to challenge assumptions.
5. Support: Transformational leaders provide support and encouragement to their followers, and they are often seen as mentors or coaches.

Transformational leaders also focus on developing the potential of their followers and creating a culture of innovation and creativity. They are often characterized by their ability to build strong relationships with their followers and to create a sense of shared ownership and responsibility for achieving the organization's goals.

Transformational theory has been the subject of much research and has been shown to be an effective approach to leadership in many different contexts. Studies have found that transformational leaders are associated with higher levels of employee motivation, job satisfaction, and organizational commitment.

Despite its strengths, transformational theory has been criticized for its lack of clarity and for its emphasis on the leader's role in creating change. Critics have argued that the theory does not adequately address the role of situational factors or the role of followers in creating change.

In response to these criticisms, some researchers have proposed more nuanced approaches to transformational theory that take into account the role of situational factors and the complex interactions between leaders and followers.

Conclusion:

Leadership is a critical aspect of human society, and its impact can be seen in every aspect of our lives. Effective leaders have the ability to inspire and influence individuals and groups towards a common goal, and throughout history, there have been many examples of great leaders who have made a significant impact on the world. There are many different theories of leadership, each of which offers a unique perspective on the nature of leadership and the qualities that make a good leader. By understanding the foundations of leadership, we can develop our own leadership skills and become more effective leaders in our own lives.

2

Understanding Leadership Styles: Autocratic, Democratic, Laissez-faire, and Situational

Leadership styles refer to the different approaches and methods that leaders use to manage and guide their team. Each leadership style has its own strengths and weaknesses, and a good leader will be able to adapt their style to suit the needs of their team and situation. In this article, we will explore four common leadership styles: Autocratic, Democratic, Laissez-faire, and Situational.

1. Autocratic Leadership Style: Autocratic leadership is a style where the leader holds all the power and makes decisions on their own. They tend to be very directive and don't seek input or feedback from their team. This style can be effective in situations where decisions need to be made quickly and decisively, or when the leader has a high level of expertise in a particular area. However, it can also lead to low morale and lack of engagement from the team, as they may feel undervalued and excluded from the decision-making process.
2. Democratic Leadership Style: Democratic leadership is a style where the leader encourages participation and input from the team when making

decisions. This style can be very effective in situations where the team has a high level of expertise or when there is a need for collaboration and creativity. It can also lead to higher levels of job satisfaction and engagement from the team, as they feel valued and heard. However, this style can also be time-consuming and may not be effective when quick decisions need to be made.

3. Laissez-faire Leadership Style: Laissez-faire leadership is a style where the leader takes a hands-off approach and allows the team to make decisions and manage themselves. This style can be effective in situations where the team is highly skilled and motivated, and where there is a high level of trust between the leader and team. It can also allow for creativity and innovation. However, this style can also lead to a lack of direction and accountability, which can result in low productivity and a lack of focus.

4. Situational Leadership Style: Situational leadership is a style where the leader adapts their approach based on the situation and needs of the team. This style can be very effective in situations where different team members have different levels of experience or skills. The leader will adjust their level of direction and support based on the needs of the individual team member. This can lead to higher levels of engagement and productivity from the team, as they feel supported and challenged in their work.

In conclusion, understanding different leadership styles is important for leaders who want to be effective in managing their team. By being aware of the strengths and weaknesses of each style, a leader can adapt their approach to suit the needs of the situation and team, ultimately leading to better outcomes for everyone involved.

3

The Qualities of a Leader: Character, Vision, Communication, and Decision-making

Leadership is the ability to inspire and guide a group of individuals towards a common goal or vision. While there are many different styles and approaches to leadership, certain qualities are universally recognized as essential for effective leadership. These qualities include character, vision, communication, and decision-making.

Character: Leadership is not just about what you do, but who you are. Character refers to the collection of traits and qualities that define an individual's moral and ethical values, and it plays a crucial role in determining whether someone is fit to lead. A leader with strong character is honest, trustworthy, dependable, and consistent in their behavior. They have integrity and are willing to stand up for their beliefs, even when it's difficult or unpopular. They treat others with respect and empathy, and they prioritize the greater good over their own interests. When a leader has strong character, they can inspire trust and loyalty among their followers, which is essential for achieving any goal.

Vision: A leader must have a clear and compelling vision of what they want to achieve. This vision should be both aspirational and realistic, inspiring people to strive for something greater while also being grounded in practicality. A good leader communicates their vision clearly and regularly to their team, ensuring that everyone is aligned around the same goals. They also have a plan for how to achieve that vision, breaking it down into actionable steps and setting clear expectations for everyone involved. With a strong vision and a clear plan, a leader can motivate their team to work together towards a common goal.

Communication: Effective communication is essential for any leader. This includes both speaking and listening skills. A leader who can articulate their vision clearly, convey their expectations, and provide constructive feedback will be able to build a strong and cohesive team. They also need to be able to listen to feedback from their team members, address concerns, and adapt their approach as necessary. Communication also involves being transparent and honest, especially when it comes to difficult decisions or challenges. When a leader communicates effectively, they can build trust and establish a culture of open communication, which is critical for achieving success.

Decision-making: Leadership often involves making tough decisions, and a good leader must be able to make them confidently and efficiently. This requires a combination of analytical thinking, intuition, and the ability to weigh risks and benefits. A leader must also be willing to take responsibility for their decisions, even when they don't turn out as expected. They should also be willing to learn from their mistakes and adjust their approach accordingly. When a leader makes good decisions, it inspires confidence and trust among their followers, which is essential for achieving success.

In conclusion, leadership requires a combination of many different qualities, including character, vision, communication, and decision-making. A leader who possesses these qualities can inspire and guide their team towards a common goal, while also building trust and a sense of shared purpose. Whether in business, politics, or any other field, effective leadership is essential for achieving success.

4

Developing Leadership Skills: Emotional Intelligence, Problem-solving, and Time Management

Developing leadership skills is a continuous process that involves honing different abilities and competencies, such as emotional intelligence, problem-solving, and time management. Effective leaders are not born; they develop their leadership skills through experience, training, and self-reflection.

One of the essential leadership skills is emotional intelligence (EI). EI refers to the ability to understand and manage one's emotions and those of others. Leaders with high EI can navigate complex interpersonal situations and communicate effectively with their team members.

Emotional intelligence (EI) is the ability to identify, understand, and manage one's own emotions, as well as the emotions of others. It is a crucial aspect of human psychology, influencing how individuals perceive and interact with the world around them. The concept of emotional intelligence was introduced in the 1990s by psychologists John Mayer and Peter Salovey, and it has since been extensively studied and applied in various fields, including education, business, and healthcare.

There are several components of emotional intelligence, including:

1. Self-awareness: This refers to the ability to recognize and understand one's own emotions, strengths, weaknesses, and motivations. People with high self-awareness are better able to manage their emotions and make decisions that align with their values and goals.
2. Self-regulation: This involves the ability to control one's own emotions and impulses, and to adapt to changing circumstances. People with strong self-regulation skills are better able to handle stress, resist temptation, and remain focused on their goals.
3. Motivation: This refers to the ability to set and achieve goals, and to persist in the face of challenges and setbacks. People with high levels of motivation are more likely to be resilient and achieve success.
4. Empathy: This involves the ability to understand and relate to the emotions and experiences of others. People with high levels of empathy are better able to build positive relationships and resolve conflicts.
5. Social skills: This refers to the ability to communicate effectively, collaborate with others, and manage relationships. People with strong social skills are more likely to be successful in their personal and professional lives.

Emotional intelligence can be developed and improved through practice and experience. Some strategies for enhancing emotional intelligence include:

1. Self-reflection: Take time to reflect on your emotions, behaviors, and thought patterns. Consider how your actions affect others and how you can improve your interactions with others.
2. Mindfulness: Practice being present in the moment and paying attention to your thoughts and feelings without judgment. This can help you develop greater self-awareness and emotional regulation skills.
3. Active listening: Listen to others with an open mind and without judgment. Try to understand their perspective and emotions, and respond with empathy and understanding.

4. Conflict resolution: Practice effective communication skills and strategies for resolving conflicts in a constructive and respectful manner.
5. Seek feedback: Ask for feedback from others on your emotional intelligence skills and areas for improvement. Use this feedback to guide your personal growth and development.

To develop emotional intelligence, leaders can engage in self-reflection and identify their strengths and weaknesses. They can also seek feedback from others, practice active listening, and demonstrate empathy towards their team members. Leaders can also engage in activities that promote self-awareness and emotional regulation, such as meditation, mindfulness, or yoga.

Another critical leadership skill is problem-solving. Leaders must be able to identify problems, evaluate different options, and make sound decisions. Problem-solving involves critical thinking, creativity, and collaboration.

To develop problem-solving skills, leaders can practice brainstorming sessions, encourage diverse perspectives and ideas, and create a culture of experimentation and learning. Leaders can also use different problem-solving frameworks, such as the Six Thinking Hats or the SCAMPER technique, to approach problems systematically and generate new solutions.

SCAMPER is a technique used to stimulate creative thinking and generate new ideas. It is an acronym for Substitute, Combine, Adapt, Modify, Put to another use, Eliminate, and Reverse. This technique was developed by Bob Eberle and was first introduced in his book "SCAMPER: Creative Games and Activities for Imagination Development" in 1971.

Each letter of the SCAMPER acronym represents a different type of question to ask yourself when generating new ideas:

1. Substitute: What can you substitute in the current idea to create something new? Can you replace one material with another, one process with another, or one component with another?
2. Combine: Can you combine different ideas, components or processes to create something new? Can you merge two or more existing ideas into one?

3. Adapt: Can you adapt an existing idea to fit a new context? Can you use an existing process in a new way or modify an existing component to better suit your needs?
4. Modify: Can you modify an existing idea to make it better? Can you change the size, shape, color, or any other feature of an existing idea to create something new?
5. Put to another use: Can you find a new use for an existing idea? Can you take an existing product or process and apply it to a new industry or market?
6. Eliminate: Can you eliminate any unnecessary components or steps from an existing idea? Can you simplify an existing process by removing any non-essential elements?
7. Reverse: Can you turn an existing idea on its head? Can you reverse the order of a process or flip the function of a component to create something new?

SCAMPER can be used in a variety of contexts, including business, education, and personal creativity. It is a simple and flexible technique that can be used by individuals or teams to generate new ideas and problem-solve in a structured and systematic way.

To use SCAMPER, simply start by asking yourself a question based on one of the seven categories above, and then brainstorm ideas based on your answers. Keep asking questions and generating new ideas until you find a solution that works for you. With practice, SCAMPER can become a powerful tool for sparking creativity and innovation.

Finally, time management is another essential leadership skill. Leaders must be able to prioritize tasks, manage their time effectively, and meet deadlines. Time management involves planning, delegation, and communication.

To develop time management skills, leaders can create a daily or weekly schedule, use time management tools, such as calendars or to-do lists, and delegate tasks to team members. Leaders can also use techniques, such as the

Pomodoro Technique, to improve their focus and productivity.

The Pomodoro Technique is a time management method that aims to increase productivity by breaking down work into short, focused intervals, followed by brief breaks. The technique was developed by Francesco Cirillo in the late 1980s and takes its name from the Italian word for "tomato" because Cirillo used a tomato-shaped kitchen timer to track his work intervals.

The Pomodoro Technique involves working in intervals of 25 minutes, known as "pomodoros," followed by a five-minute break. After completing four consecutive pomodoros, a longer break of 15-30 minutes is taken. During the break, it's important to step away from work and engage in a different activity to rest and refresh your mind.

To start using the Pomodoro Technique, follow these steps:

1. Choose a task to work on.
2. Set the timer for 25 minutes.
3. Work on the task until the timer rings.
4. Take a five-minute break.
5. Repeat the process, taking a longer break after every four pomodoros.

The Pomodoro Technique can be applied to a wide range of tasks, from writing and studying to programming and designing. It's particularly helpful for tasks that require sustained focus, as it helps to break up the work into manageable chunks and provides built-in breaks for rest and reflection.

One of the key benefits of the Pomodoro Technique is that it helps to minimize distractions and improve concentration. By working in short intervals, you're less likely to get distracted by external factors like social media or email notifications. Instead, you can fully immerse yourself in the task at hand and make steady progress towards your goals.

Another benefit of the Pomodoro Technique is that it helps to combat procrastination. By breaking tasks into smaller, more manageable pieces, it can be easier to get started and build momentum. Additionally, the technique provides a sense of structure and accountability, making it easier to stay on track and avoid distractions.

Overall, the Pomodoro Technique is a simple but effective time management method that can help you work more efficiently and productively. By breaking tasks into short intervals and taking regular breaks, you can maintain focus and motivation, minimize distractions, and make steady progress towards your goals.

In conclusion, developing leadership skills is a continuous process that requires self-reflection, practice, and learning. Emotional intelligence, problem-solving, and time management are critical skills that effective leaders must possess. By focusing on these skills and engaging in different activities, leaders can improve their performance and drive success in their organizations.

5

Leading Teams: Building Trust, Motivating, and Delegating Responsibilities

Leading teams is a crucial aspect of effective leadership. When leading a team, it is important to build trust, motivate team members, and delegate responsibilities. In this response, we will discuss each of these three elements in detail.

Building Trust:

Building trust is a foundational element of leading a successful team. Trust is developed through open communication, transparency, and consistency. Leaders should be clear in their expectations and provide regular feedback to their team members. This helps team members to understand their role and how their work contributes to the overall goals of the team.

Trust is an essential aspect of any successful team. When team members trust each other, they work more effectively, communicate more openly, and are more willing to collaborate. However, building trust within a team can be a challenging task, particularly if the team members are new to each other or have had negative experiences in the past.

One way a leader can build trust in their team is by introducing trust games. These games are designed to promote communication, collaboration, and empathy among team members. Here are a few trust games that a leader can introduce in their team:

1. The Trust Fall: In this game, a team member stands on a chair or a raised platform while the rest of the team stands below. The team member then falls backward, trusting that their teammates will catch them before they hit the ground. This game helps build trust by requiring team members to rely on each other.
2. Blindfolded Obstacle Course: In this game, team members are divided into pairs. One team member is blindfolded, and the other team member guides them through an obstacle course without touching them. This game helps build trust by requiring team members to rely on each other's communication and problem-solving skills.
3. Two Truths and a Lie: In this game, each team member shares three statements about themselves, two of which are true, and one of which is a lie. The rest of the team has to guess which statement is a lie. This game helps build trust by encouraging team members to share personal information with each other and getting to know each other better.
4. The Human Knot: In this game, team members stand in a circle, and everyone puts their hands in the center. Each person grabs two random hands from the center, creating a human knot. The team then has to work together to untangle the knot without letting go of each other's hands. This game helps build trust by requiring team members to communicate, collaborate, and rely on each other.
5. Building Blocks: In this game, team members are divided into pairs. One team member is given a set of building blocks and has to build a structure without showing their partner the blocks. The other team member has to recreate the structure without being able to see it. This game helps build trust by requiring team members to communicate clearly and trust that their partner will accurately recreate the structure.

Additionally, leaders should be honest and transparent with their team members. This means sharing information about the team's objectives, challenges, and successes. By being open and honest, leaders can establish a culture of trust within the team.

Motivating:

Motivating team members is another important aspect of leading a successful team. Leaders should understand what motivates each team member and use this knowledge to create a positive and productive work environment. This can include providing opportunities for growth and development, recognizing and rewarding good performance, and creating a sense of ownership and accountability among team members.

Motivation games are a fun and engaging way for leaders to build morale and motivation among their team. These games can help team members feel more connected to each other and the mission of the organization, and can also increase productivity and creativity. Here are some motivation games that a leader can introduce in his team:

1. Scavenger Hunt: A scavenger hunt is a great way to build teamwork and problem-solving skills. The leader can create a list of items or tasks that the team needs to find or complete, and the team must work together to accomplish the goals. This game can be done indoors or outdoors, and can be customized to fit the needs of the team.
2. Brain Teasers: Brain teasers are a fun way to challenge team members to think creatively and outside of the box. The leader can provide puzzles, riddles, or other brain teasers for the team to solve, and the team can work together to come up with the answers. This game can be done individually or in groups, and can be adjusted to fit the skill level of the team.
3. Game Day: A game day is a fun way to boost morale and build camaraderie among team members. The leader can choose a variety of games to play, such as board games, card games, or video games, and the team can compete against each other in a friendly and supportive environment. This game can be done during a lunch break or after work hours.

4. Storytelling: Storytelling is a powerful tool for building connections and creating a shared sense of purpose. The leader can ask team members to share stories about their personal or professional lives, and the team can listen and provide feedback. This game can be done in a group setting or one-on-one, and can help team members feel more connected and understood.
5. Goal Setting: Goal setting is an important part of motivation, as it gives team members a clear sense of direction and purpose. The leader can ask team members to set individual or team goals, and the team can work together to achieve them. This game can be done in a brainstorming session or during a team meeting.

One effective way to motivate team members is to set clear goals and expectations. When team members understand what is expected of them, they are more likely to be motivated to achieve those goals. Leaders can also provide regular feedback and recognition to their team members to help them stay motivated and engaged.

Delegating Responsibilities:

Delegating responsibilities is another critical element of leading a successful team. Leaders should understand the strengths and weaknesses of each team member and delegate tasks accordingly. By delegating responsibilities effectively, leaders can create a more efficient and productive team.

When delegating responsibilities, it is important to provide clear instructions and expectations. This helps team members to understand their role and what is expected of them. Additionally, leaders should provide support and resources to their team members to help them successfully complete their tasks.

In conclusion, leading a successful team requires building trust, motivating team members, and delegating responsibilities effectively. By focusing on these three elements, leaders can create a positive and productive work environment that supports the success of the team.

6

Managing Conflict: Strategies for Resolving Disputes and Overcoming Obstacles

Managing conflict is an essential skill in both personal and professional settings. Conflicts can arise from a variety of sources, including differences in values, priorities, and communication styles, as well as competing goals and interests. However, conflicts can be managed effectively through the use of various strategies for resolving disputes and overcoming obstacles.

One of the most effective strategies for managing conflict is active listening. This involves actively engaging with the other person, asking questions, and seeking to understand their perspective. By demonstrating empathy and actively listening to the other person's point of view, it is possible to defuse tensions and find common ground.

Another key strategy for managing conflict is collaboration. Collaboration involves working together with the other person to find a mutually beneficial solution to the problem. This may involve brainstorming ideas, negotiating a compromise, or finding creative ways to meet both parties' needs. Collaboration can be particularly effective when both parties have a vested interest in the outcome.

Active listening is a communication skill that involves fully engaging with the speaker, understanding their perspective, and responding appropriately. It requires a conscious effort to pay attention to what someone is saying, understand their point of view, and respond in a way that shows you understand what they are saying. In this article, we will explore in detail how to practice active listening.

1. Focus on the speaker: One of the most important aspects of active listening is to focus on the speaker. Give them your undivided attention by putting away distractions like your phone or computer. Make eye contact, and face them directly, leaning in slightly to show that you are engaged and interested in what they have to say.
2. Avoid interrupting: Interrupting the speaker can be frustrating and may disrupt their thought process. Instead of interrupting, wait until they have finished speaking before responding. If you need to ask for clarification or have a question, wait for an appropriate pause and then ask.
3. Use body language to show engagement: Non-verbal cues like nodding your head, smiling, and making eye contact show the speaker that you are engaged and listening. Avoid crossing your arms or looking away as these may send signals that you are disinterested or defensive.
4. Paraphrase and summarize: To ensure that you understand what the speaker is saying, paraphrase their statements in your own words. This technique helps to clarify the speaker's message and demonstrates that you are paying attention. Summarizing what they've said can also help to confirm your understanding and show that you're invested in their message.
5. Ask open-ended questions: Open-ended questions encourage the speaker to share more about their thoughts and feelings. These types of questions can start with phrases such as "Can you tell me more about that?" or "How did that make you feel?" This approach can help to deepen the conversation and foster a more meaningful dialogue.
6. Avoid judgment or assumptions: As an active listener, it is important

to remain impartial and avoid making assumptions or judgments about the speaker or their message. Keep an open mind and be willing to consider multiple perspectives. By doing this, you will create a safe and supportive environment for the speaker to share their thoughts and feelings.
7. Respond appropriately: Once the speaker has finished sharing their thoughts, respond appropriately. You can acknowledge what they have shared by expressing empathy, validating their feelings, or offering support. Avoid offering unsolicited advice or attempting to solve their problems unless asked to do so.

In some cases, compromise may be necessary to manage conflict. Compromise involves both parties giving up something in order to reach a mutually acceptable solution. This may involve finding a middle ground or agreeing to a partial solution. Compromise can be an effective strategy when the parties involved have fundamentally different values or priorities.

Compromise is a vital aspect of leadership, particularly when it comes to achieving the greater good for an organization, community, or society at large. A leader who can arrive at a compromise can effectively manage conflicts, build alliances, and foster collaboration, ultimately leading to successful outcomes. In this article, we will discuss how a leader can arrive at a compromise for the sake of the greater good.

1. Identify the Goals: The first step in arriving at a compromise is to identify the goals that need to be achieved. It is important to understand the objectives of all parties involved in the negotiation. A leader should ensure that they have a clear understanding of what is at stake and what each party is trying to accomplish.
2. Identify Common Ground: Once the goals are identified, a leader should identify the areas of common ground. This is where the parties can work together to achieve their goals. Identifying common ground can help build trust, improve communication, and create a foundation for a

compromise.

3. Understand the Differences: In any negotiation, there are bound to be differences in opinion. A leader should understand these differences and try to find ways to bridge the gap. Understanding the differences can help the leader find ways to meet the needs of all parties involved.
4. Brainstorm Solutions: Once the goals are identified, common ground is established, and differences are understood, a leader can begin to brainstorm solutions. This is where the parties involved can come up with ideas and suggestions that can lead to a compromise. Brainstorming solutions can help the leader to come up with innovative ideas that can benefit everyone involved.
5. Evaluate the Solutions: After brainstorming solutions, the leader should evaluate them to determine which ones are feasible and which ones are not. It is important to evaluate the solutions objectively and determine which ones will provide the greatest benefit to all parties involved.
6. Implement the Compromise: Once a compromise is agreed upon, the leader should implement it. It is important to communicate the compromise to all parties involved and ensure that everyone is aware of their roles and responsibilities. A leader should also ensure that the compromise is enforced and that all parties involved are held accountable for their actions.
7. Evaluate the Compromise: After the compromise is implemented, a leader should evaluate its effectiveness. This is where the leader can determine whether the compromise achieved the goals that were set out at the beginning of the negotiation. If the compromise was successful, the leader can use it as a model for future negotiations.

When conflicts cannot be resolved through collaboration or compromise, it may be necessary to escalate the conflict to a higher authority. This may involve bringing in a third party, such as a mediator or arbitrator, to help facilitate a resolution. A third party can provide an objective perspective and help both parties find a mutually acceptable solution.

Finally, it is important to recognize when conflicts cannot be resolved and to accept that some conflicts may need to be managed rather than resolved. This may involve finding ways to minimize the impact of the conflict, such as by setting boundaries or agreeing to disagree. Managing conflicts can be particularly important in situations where there is a power imbalance or where the conflict involves deeply held beliefs or values.

In conclusion, managing conflict is an important skill that can be learned and developed over time. By actively listening, collaborating, compromising, escalating to a higher authority when necessary, and managing conflicts that cannot be resolved, individuals can effectively manage conflicts and overcome obstacles. With practice, these strategies can become second nature, helping to prevent conflicts from escalating and fostering positive relationships with others.

7

Building a Culture of Accountability: Setting Expectations, Providing Feedback, and Celebrating Success

Building a culture of accountability is essential for any organization to achieve its goals and objectives. It involves setting clear expectations, providing regular feedback, and celebrating success. In this article, we will delve deeper into these three key components of accountability and explore how they can help create a culture of responsibility and ownership within a team or organization.

Setting Expectations:

Setting clear expectations is the foundation of accountability. When people know what is expected of them, they are more likely to take ownership of their work and be accountable for their results. This starts with setting SMART (Specific, Measurable, Achievable, Relevant, and Time-bound) goals and objectives for the team or individual. These goals should be aligned with the organization's vision and mission.

SMART goals are specific, measurable, achievable, relevant, and time-bound goals that provide a framework for individuals and organizations to set and achieve their objectives. The SMART acronym is used to guide the goal-setting process, ensuring that goals are specific, quantifiable, and meaningful, while also being realistic and time-bound.

Let's break down the SMART acronym and examine each component in detail:

1. Specific: Goals should be specific and clearly defined. This means that they should be well-defined and unambiguous, leaving no room for confusion or misinterpretation. Specific goals answer the questions "what", "why", "who", "where" and "when".

For example, instead of setting a vague goal like "increase sales", a specific goal would be "increase sales of product X by 10% by the end of the quarter".

1. Measurable: Goals should be measurable so that progress can be tracked and success can be determined. This means that the goal should be quantifiable, with a clear way to measure progress and success.

For example, instead of setting a goal to "improve customer satisfaction", a measurable goal would be "increase customer satisfaction scores by 20% in the next 6 months through surveys and feedback forms".

1. Achievable: Goals should be achievable, meaning that they should be challenging but also realistic and attainable. Goals should be set based on an individual's or organization's capabilities, resources, and skills.

For example, setting a goal to increase sales by 1000% in a month when there are limited resources and market conditions are not favorable is not achievable. Instead, a more achievable goal would be to increase sales by 10% in the next quarter.

1. Relevant: Goals should be relevant and aligned with an individual's or organization's overall mission, vision, and values. Relevant goals help an individual or organization move closer to their overall objectives.

For example, setting a goal to increase sales of a product that is not aligned with the company's overall mission or values is not relevant. Instead, setting a goal to increase sales of a product that aligns with the company's mission and values is relevant.

1. Time-bound: Goals should be time-bound, meaning that they should have a deadline or timeframe for completion. Time-bound goals provide a sense of urgency and accountability, and help individuals or organizations stay on track.

For example, setting a goal to increase sales by 10% is not time-bound. Instead, setting a goal to increase sales by 10% in the next quarter provides a specific deadline for completion.

Overall, SMART goals provide a framework for setting and achieving objectives that are specific, measurable, achievable, relevant, and time-bound. By following this framework, individuals and organizations can set goals that are challenging, yet attainable, and move closer to achieving their overall objectives.

Communicating these expectations clearly is also crucial. It is not enough to simply set goals and objectives; you must ensure that everyone understands what is expected of them. This can be achieved by having regular team meetings, one-on-one discussions, and using performance management tools such as KPIs (Key Performance Indicators) to track progress and provide ongoing feedback.

Providing Feedback:

Feedback is an essential part of accountability. It provides people with an understanding of how they are performing and helps them make adjustments to achieve their goals. Regular feedback helps to build trust and foster a culture of open communication within the team.

Feedback should be constructive, timely, and specific. It should focus on behavior and performance, not on the person. When providing feedback, it is essential to recognize what has been done well, and identify areas for improvement. This should be followed up with support and resources to help individuals or teams achieve their goals.

Celebrating Success:

Celebrating success is a vital component of building a culture of accountability. Recognizing and celebrating progress, milestones, and achievements motivates people to continue striving for excellence. Celebrating success also helps to reinforce the values and behaviors that lead to success and fosters a positive team culture.

Celebrations do not have to be big events; they can be as simple as a team lunch or a thank-you note. It is important to celebrate not only the big wins but also the small achievements along the way. This helps to build momentum and maintain motivation.

In conclusion, building a culture of accountability is essential for achieving organizational goals and creating a positive team culture. It involves setting clear expectations, providing regular feedback, and celebrating success. When these components are integrated into the fabric of an organization, they help to create a sense of ownership, responsibility, and commitment among team members. As a result, individuals and teams are more likely to take ownership of their work, be accountable for their results, and contribute to the success of the organization.

8

Leading Change: Planning and Implementing Organizational Change, and Managing Resistance

Leading change is a critical skill for leaders and managers in organizations today. As organizations grow and evolve, they must adapt to changes in the business environment to remain competitive and achieve their goals. Change can take many forms, such as introducing new technology, reorganizing the company structure, or implementing new processes and procedures. However, implementing change is not always easy, and many organizations face resistance from employees or other stakeholders.

Planning and implementing organizational change involves a structured process that requires careful planning, communication, and collaboration. The process typically includes the following steps:

1. Identify the need for change: The first step in planning and implementing organizational change is to identify the need for change. This could be due to a shift in the business environment, changes in customer demands, or internal issues within the organization.
2. Develop a change management plan: Once the need for change has been identified, it is essential to develop a change management plan. This plan

should outline the objectives of the change, the stakeholders involved, the resources required, and the timeline for implementation.
3. Communicate the change: Communication is critical in any change management initiative. Leaders must communicate the need for change, the objectives of the change, and the benefits it will bring to the organization. Communication should be frequent, transparent, and consistent.
4. Build a coalition of support: Building a coalition of support is essential to implementing successful change. This involves identifying key stakeholders, including employees, customers, and suppliers, and gaining their support for the change initiative.
5. Implement the change: Once the plan is in place, and support has been gained, it is time to implement the change. This may involve introducing new technology, reorganizing the company structure, or changing processes and procedures.
6. Monitor and evaluate the change: After implementing the change, it is essential to monitor and evaluate its effectiveness. This involves measuring the results and assessing whether the change has achieved the desired outcomes.

Managing resistance is a critical aspect of planning and implementing organizational change. Resistance to change is a natural human response and can occur for many reasons, including fear of the unknown, a lack of trust in leadership, and concerns about job security. However, if resistance is not managed effectively, it can derail the change initiative and prevent the organization from achieving its goals.

To manage resistance effectively, leaders should:

- Anticipate resistance: Leaders should anticipate resistance and be prepared to address it. This involves identifying potential sources of resistance and developing strategies to manage them.

Leadership is about taking people from a current state to a future state, often in the face of resistance or opposition. Resistance is a natural reaction to change, and anticipating it is crucial for a leader to implement change effectively. Anticipating resistance enables leaders to prepare in advance, identify potential barriers, and find ways to overcome them.

Here are some ways a leader can anticipate resistance and find ways to overcome them:

1. Assess potential resistance: The first step in anticipating resistance is to assess it. Leaders should identify who might resist change and why they might do so. This involves analyzing their beliefs, attitudes, and behaviors. For example, employees who have been with the company for a long time may resist changes that they perceive as a threat to their job security. By identifying potential resistance, a leader can tailor their approach to address the specific concerns of those who may resist change.
2. Communicate effectively: Effective communication is crucial to overcoming resistance to change. Leaders should be transparent about the reasons for the change, the benefits it will bring, and the potential impact on employees. This will help to build trust and create a sense of shared purpose. A leader should also listen to employees' concerns and address them in a way that shows empathy and understanding.
3. Create a shared vision: A leader should create a shared vision of the future state that the change will bring. This will help employees to understand the big picture and see how their work contributes to the overall goal. When employees have a clear understanding of the vision, they are more likely to support the change.
4. Build a coalition of support: A leader should build a coalition of support for the change. This involves identifying key stakeholders who can help to influence others and bring them on board. Leaders should also identify potential champions who can advocate for the change and help to overcome resistance.
5. Provide training and resources: Resistance to change can often be overcome by providing training and resources to employees. This will

help them to develop the skills they need to adapt to the change and be successful in their new roles. It can also help to alleviate any fears or concerns that they may have about the change.
6. Celebrate successes: Celebrating successes along the way can help to build momentum and create a sense of progress. A leader should recognize and reward employees who are making progress and achieving results. This will help to create a positive culture and reinforce the benefits of the change.
7. Monitor progress: Finally, a leader should monitor progress and adjust their approach as needed. This involves measuring the impact of the change, identifying areas for improvement, and making adjustments to ensure the change is successful in the long term.

- Communicate the benefits: Effective communication is critical in managing resistance. Leaders should communicate the benefits of the change initiative and how it will positively impact the organization and its stakeholders.
- Address concerns: Leaders should address concerns about the change initiative and provide reassurance to employees. This could involve providing training and support to employees, offering job security, or addressing any other concerns that employees may have.
- Involve employees: Involving employees in the change initiative can help to manage resistance. Leaders should encourage employee participation and seek their input on how the change can be implemented effectively.
- Celebrate successes: Celebrating successes can help to build momentum and maintain employee motivation during the change initiative. Leaders should acknowledge the achievements of employees and the progress made towards achieving the objectives of the change initiative.

In conclusion, planning and implementing organizational change is a critical skill for leaders and managers in organizations. Effective change management involves a structured process, clear communication, collaboration, and the ability to manage resistance. By following a structured approach and addressing resistance effectively, leaders can successfully implement change initiatives and achieve the desired outcomes for their organization.

9

Ethics and Values: Balancing Personal and Organizational Values, and Ethical Decision-making

Ethics and values are fundamental concepts that guide the behavior and decision-making of individuals and organizations. Ethics refers to the moral principles and values that guide human behavior, while values are the beliefs, attitudes, and principles that individuals and organizations hold dear. Ethics and values are closely related, as ethical behavior is based on a set of shared values that are agreed upon within a community or organization.

Balancing personal and organizational values is an important aspect of ethical decision-making. Individuals may have personal values that conflict with the values of their organization, and this can create ethical dilemmas. For example, an employee may have a personal value of honesty, but the organizational culture may encourage employees to withhold information from clients to maintain a competitive advantage. In such situations, individuals must make a choice between their personal values and the values of the organization.

One approach to balancing personal and organizational values is to engage in ethical reasoning. This involves a process of reflection and critical thinking that helps individuals to identify and evaluate ethical dilemmas and to make decisions that are consistent with their values. Ethical reasoning involves considering the consequences of one's actions, as well as the principles and values that guide those actions.

Ethical decision-making involves a process of weighing the pros and cons of different courses of action and choosing the course that is most consistent with one's values and ethical principles. This process can be complex and challenging, as it often involves balancing competing interests and values. In making ethical decisions, individuals must consider the impact of their actions on stakeholders, including customers, employees, shareholders, and the broader community.

One framework for ethical decision-making is the four-component model, which includes the following steps:

- Ethical Awareness: Recognizing the ethical issue at hand and the potential impact of various decisions on stakeholders.

Ethical awareness is a crucial aspect of leadership that involves understanding the principles and values that guide ethical behavior. It refers to the ability of a leader to identify ethical dilemmas, evaluate the consequences of different actions, and make ethical decisions. Leaders who are ethically aware have a strong sense of responsibility towards their stakeholders and are committed to upholding ethical standards in their decision-making processes.

Here are some key aspects of ethical awareness that are important for a leader:

1. Understanding ethical principles: A leader should be familiar with ethical principles such as fairness, justice, respect for others, integrity, and accountability. They should understand how these principles apply to different situations and be able to identify ethical dilemmas.
2. Developing ethical reasoning skills: Leaders should be able to use ethical reasoning to evaluate different options when faced with ethical dilemmas. They should consider the potential consequences of different

actions and weigh the interests of different stakeholders to make an ethical decision.
3. Creating a culture of ethics: A leader should foster a culture of ethics within their organization by promoting ethical behavior and making it clear that unethical behavior will not be tolerated. They should also provide guidance and support to their team members to help them navigate ethical dilemmas.
4. Communicating ethical values: Leaders should communicate their ethical values and expectations to their team members and stakeholders. This includes setting ethical standards, explaining the rationale behind ethical decisions, and providing training and resources to support ethical behavior.
5. Leading by example: A leader should model ethical behavior in their actions and decisions. They should demonstrate a commitment to ethical values and hold themselves accountable for their actions.

- Ethical Judgment: Assessing the situation from various perspectives and evaluating the options available.

Ethical judgment is a critical component of effective leadership. It refers to the ability of a leader to make sound ethical decisions based on a set of principles and values. Ethical judgment involves evaluating the potential consequences of different actions, considering the interests of different stakeholders, and making decisions that align with ethical principles. Here are some key aspects of ethical judgment that are important for a leader:

1. Understanding ethical principles: A leader should have a strong understanding of ethical principles such as integrity, accountability, fairness, and respect for others. They should be familiar with the relevant ethical standards in their field and be able to apply them to different situations.
2. Assessing ethical risks: A leader should be able to identify potential ethical risks and evaluate their potential impact on different stakeholders. They should consider the potential consequences of different actions

and weigh the interests of different stakeholders to make an ethical decision.
3. Considering the context: A leader should take into account the context of a situation when making ethical judgments. They should consider factors such as cultural norms, legal requirements, and organizational policies that may influence the decision-making process.
4. Using ethical reasoning: A leader should use ethical reasoning to evaluate different options when faced with ethical dilemmas. They should consider the potential consequences of different actions and weigh the interests of different stakeholders to make an ethical decision.
5. Seeking guidance: A leader should seek guidance from ethical experts, mentors, and other resources when faced with complex ethical dilemmas. They should also consult with stakeholders and seek their input to ensure that their decision is aligned with their interests.
6. Reflecting on past decisions: A leader should reflect on past decisions and consider the outcomes of their decisions in light of ethical principles. They should be willing to learn from their mistakes and make adjustments to their decision-making processes.

- Ethical Intent: Choosing the course of action that is most consistent with one's values and ethical principles.

Ethical intent is a crucial aspect of effective leadership that involves a leader's commitment to act in accordance with ethical principles and values. Ethical intent refers to the leader's intention to do what is right and ethical, regardless of the potential consequences. Here are some key aspects of ethical intent that are important for a leader:

1. Commitment to ethical principles: A leader with ethical intent is committed to ethical principles such as integrity, accountability, fairness, and respect for others. They are guided by a strong sense of moral responsibility and prioritize ethical considerations in their decision-making processes.

2. Transparency and openness: A leader with ethical intent is transparent and open in their communication with stakeholders. They share information openly, seek feedback, and are willing to admit mistakes and take responsibility for their actions.
3. Consistency in behavior: A leader with ethical intent is consistent in their behavior, demonstrating ethical principles consistently in their actions and decisions. They set a positive example for their team members by modeling ethical behavior.
4. Empathy and compassion: A leader with ethical intent demonstrates empathy and compassion towards others. They take into account the interests and needs of different stakeholders and consider the potential impact of their decisions on them.
5. Continuous improvement: A leader with ethical intent is committed to continuous improvement and learning. They seek feedback and input from others, reflect on their decisions, and take steps to improve their decision-making processes.
6. Emphasis on long-term goals: A leader with ethical intent focuses on long-term goals and sustainability rather than short-term gains. They consider the impact of their decisions on future generations and the environment.

- Ethical Behavior: Implementing the chosen course of action and taking responsibility for the consequences.

Ethical behavior is a critical aspect of effective leadership that involves acting in accordance with ethical principles and values. Ethical behavior refers to the actions and decisions of a leader that align with ethical principles and values. Here are some key aspects of ethical behavior that are important for a leader:

1. Honesty and integrity: A leader with ethical behavior is honest and transparent in their communication with stakeholders. They demonstrate integrity by adhering to ethical principles and values even when

it is difficult to do so.
2. Fairness and justice: A leader with ethical behavior treats others fairly and justly. They make decisions that consider the interests of all stakeholders and ensure that everyone is treated equitably.
3. Respect for others: A leader with ethical behavior demonstrates respect for others, regardless of their position or status. They listen to others and value their input, even if they disagree with their opinions.
4. Accountability: A leader with ethical behavior takes responsibility for their actions and decisions. They are willing to admit mistakes and take corrective action when necessary.
5. Empathy and compassion: A leader with ethical behavior demonstrates empathy and compassion towards others. They consider the impact of their decisions on different stakeholders and take steps to minimize any negative effects.
6. Consistency in behavior: A leader with ethical behavior demonstrates ethical principles consistently in their actions and decisions. They set a positive example for their team members by modeling ethical behavior.
7. Continuous improvement: A leader with ethical behavior is committed to continuous improvement and learning. They seek feedback and input from others, reflect on their decisions, and take steps to improve their decision-making processes.

Another framework for ethical decision-making is the principle-based approach, which involves applying ethical principles such as honesty, fairness, and respect for human dignity to specific situations. This approach emphasizes the importance of universal ethical principles that apply to all individuals and organizations.

In conclusion, ethics and values are essential concepts that guide the behavior and decision-making of individuals and organizations. Balancing personal and organizational values is an important aspect of ethical decision-making, and this requires reflection, critical thinking, and a commitment to ethical principles. Ethical decision-making involves a process of weighing the pros and cons of different courses of action and choosing the course that is most consistent with one's values and ethical principles. By embracing ethical behavior, individuals and organizations can build trust, foster positive relationships, and contribute to a more just and sustainable society.

10

Leadership in a Global World: Cross-cultural Communication and Understanding, and Managing Diversity

Leadership in a global world is an essential skill for individuals who are responsible for managing teams, organizations, or businesses with diverse cultural backgrounds. In a world where globalization has brought people from different regions, cultures, and languages together, it has become crucial for leaders to understand the nuances of cross-cultural communication and manage diversity effectively.

Cross-cultural communication refers to the process of exchanging information between people from different cultures. Communication is the cornerstone of leadership, and understanding cultural differences is vital to effective communication. Leaders who can effectively communicate across cultures can build relationships, avoid misunderstandings, and create a positive work environment.

Managing diversity involves understanding, respecting, and valuing differences between people in a workplace. A diverse team can bring different perspectives, ideas, and solutions to the table. A leader who can manage diversity effectively can foster an environment of inclusion and promote collaboration among team members.

To be a successful leader in a global world, it is essential to have cross-cultural communication skills and manage diversity effectively. Some key strategies that leaders can use to develop these skills include:

1. Educate Yourself: Leaders must learn about different cultures and customs to understand their team members' perspectives. Learning about different cultures can help leaders avoid misunderstandings and build stronger relationships.
2. Listen actively: Active listening involves paying attention to what the other person is saying, asking clarifying questions, and summarizing their main points. This approach helps leaders understand their team members' perspectives, build trust, and promote open communication.
3. Be Open-minded: Leaders must be open-minded and willing to learn from their team members. They should be receptive to new ideas and perspectives, even if they challenge their own beliefs and assumptions.
4. Lead by Example: Leaders must set an example of inclusion by treating everyone with respect and fairness. They should demonstrate their commitment to diversity and inclusion by promoting and supporting diverse candidates for leadership roles.
5. Foster Collaboration: Leaders should create an environment of collaboration by encouraging their team members to work together, share ideas, and solve problems collectively. This approach promotes teamwork and helps team members learn from each other's strengths and weaknesses.

In conclusion, leadership in a global world requires cross-cultural communication skills and effective diversity management. Leaders who can communicate effectively across cultures and manage diversity can build stronger relationships, foster a positive work environment, and promote collaboration among team members. By following the strategies outlined above, leaders can develop the skills they need to succeed in today's diverse and globalized workplace.

11

The Foundations of Kingship: History and Evolution of Kingship

The concept of kingship dates back to ancient times and has undergone various changes and transformations throughout history. It is a form of government where a monarch, typically a king or queen, holds absolute or limited power over a state or territory.

The origins of kingship are rooted in the social and political structures of early human societies. In many ancient civilizations, the king was seen as a divine figure or a representative of the gods, and his authority was unquestionable. The king was responsible for maintaining social order and protecting the community from external threats, such as invasion or natural disasters.

As societies grew more complex, so too did the role of the king. Kingship became more institutionalized, and the king's power was often balanced by a council of advisors or a parliament. In some societies, the king's power was limited by law, and his actions were subject to the approval of a governing body.

Throughout history, kingship has taken many different forms. In some societies, the king was an absolute ruler, with complete control over the state and its people. In other societies, the king was more of a figurehead, with limited power and authority.

One of the earliest examples of kingship can be found in ancient Egypt, where pharaohs ruled over the state for thousands of years. The pharaoh was seen as a god-king, with the power to control the Nile River, which was crucial for agriculture and transportation.

In Mesopotamia, kingship evolved from city-states, where local rulers held power over a small territory. As cities grew and kingdoms emerged, the role of the king became more important. In Babylon, Hammurabi established one of the earliest legal codes, which set out the rules for kingship and the responsibilities of the king.

In ancient Greece, kingship took on a more ceremonial role, with the king acting as a religious leader and presiding over ceremonies and festivals. The city-state of Sparta had two kings, who ruled jointly and held equal power, while in Athens, the king was replaced by a council of elected officials.

In Europe, kingship evolved from tribal societies, where local leaders held power over a small group of people. As kingdoms emerged, the role of the king became more important, and in many cases, the king was seen as a divine figure or representative of God. In medieval Europe, kingship was closely tied to the Christian Church, and the king was often seen as a defender of the faith.

In modern times, kingship has become less common, with many countries adopting forms of government that are more democratic in nature. However, there are still a number of countries that have monarchies, where the king or queen serves as a figurehead or has limited powers.

In conclusion, the concept of kingship has played a significant role in human history, evolving over time to meet the changing needs of society. While the form of kingship has varied from culture to culture and from era to era, the role of the king as a leader and protector of the people has remained a constant throughout history.

12

The Role of the King: Power, Responsibilities, and Relationships with the People

The role of the king has evolved throughout history, but regardless of the time period or culture, the king has always been a figure of great power and responsibility. In this essay, we will explore the role of the king in terms of his power, responsibilities, and relationships with the people.

Power: The king is the supreme ruler of his kingdom, and as such, he has significant power over his people. The extent of this power varies depending on the culture and time period, but in general, the king has the power to make laws, impose taxes, declare war, and make peace. He also has the power to appoint officials and judges, as well as the power to pardon or punish criminals.

Responsibilities: With great power comes great responsibility, and the king has many responsibilities to his people. First and foremost, the king is responsible for ensuring the safety and security of his kingdom. This includes defending the kingdom against external threats as well as maintaining law and order within the kingdom.

The king is also responsible for managing the economy of his kingdom. This includes overseeing the production and distribution of goods, as well as managing the tax system to ensure that the kingdom has the resources it needs to function.

In addition to these responsibilities, the king is also expected to provide for the welfare of his people. This includes ensuring that there is enough food and water for everyone, as well as providing healthcare, education, and other basic services.

Relationships with the people: The king's relationship with the people is an important aspect of his role. In many cultures, the king is seen as a father figure to his people, responsible for their well-being and protection. As such, the king is expected to be just and fair in his dealings with his people.

The king is also expected to be accessible to his people, to listen to their concerns and to address their needs. In many cultures, the king holds court regularly, where he meets with his subjects and hears their grievances. The king is also expected to be a role model for his people, embodying the values and virtues that are important to the culture.

Conclusion: In conclusion, the role of the king is one of great power, responsibility, and importance. The king is responsible for the safety, security, and well-being of his people, and he is expected to be just and fair in his dealings with them. The king's relationship with his people is an important aspect of his role, and he is expected to be accessible, to listen to his people, and to be a role model for them.

13

The Qualities of a King: Wisdom, Justice, and Courage

The concept of a king or a leader, who embodies wisdom, justice, and courage, has been central to many societies throughout history. These qualities are often seen as essential for a ruler to govern effectively and justly. Let's explore each of these qualities in more detail:

- Wisdom:

Wisdom is often described as the ability to make good decisions based on experience, knowledge, and understanding. A wise king is someone who is able to use their intellect and insight to make the best possible decisions for their people. They are able to see the big picture and think long-term, considering the consequences of their actions and decisions. A wise king is also someone who is able to learn from their mistakes and take advice from others.

A wise king is a ruler who governs his kingdom with a clear sense of purpose, wisdom, and justice. Here are some examples of wise kings throughout history:

1. King Solomon of Israel - King Solomon is known for his wisdom, which was granted to him by God. He is famous for his judgment in the case of two women who claimed to be the mother of the same child. He proposed to cut the child in half and give each woman a piece. The real mother, out of love for her child, surrendered her claim, and the baby was given to her. This wise judgment became a symbol of Solomon's wisdom and justice.
2. King Ashoka of India - King Ashoka was a Mauryan emperor who ruled India from 268 to 232 BCE. He was known for his policies of non-violence, tolerance, and religious pluralism. After a brutal war, he embraced Buddhism and dedicated his life to spreading its teachings. He built roads, hospitals, and public works for his subjects, and his policies are credited with helping to create a stable and prosperous society.
3. King Alfred the Great of England - King Alfred is known for his military and political victories against the Vikings in the late 9th century. He was also a wise ruler who promoted learning and education, commissioning translations of important works into English. He also established a legal code that was based on justice and fairness, and he worked to improve the lives of his subjects by building schools and improving the economy.
4. King Louis IX of France - King Louis IX is known for his deep piety and devotion to his faith. He was a just and fair ruler who worked to improve the lives of his subjects by passing laws that protected them from abuse and corruption. He also established hospitals and other charitable institutions to care for the poor and sick, and he is remembered for his humility and kindness.
5. King Abdullah II of Jordan - King Abdullah II is a contemporary monarch who has demonstrated wisdom and leadership in his role as ruler of Jordan. He has worked to promote peace and stability in the Middle East and has been a vocal advocate for reform and modernization in his country. He has also championed education and economic development, and his policies have helped to make Jordan a more prosperous and stable nation.

- Justice:

Justice refers to the fair and equitable treatment of all individuals. A just king is someone who upholds the law and treats all citizens equally, regardless of their social status or wealth. They ensure that everyone is treated fairly and that justice is served in all matters, whether it's in the court of law or in the distribution of resources. A just king also recognizes the importance of compassion and empathy, understanding that sometimes the strict application of the law is not always the most humane approach.

A just king is a ruler who upholds fairness, equity, and righteousness in his or her governance. Here are some detailed examples of a just king:

1. King Solomon: King Solomon is a well-known biblical figure who is admired for his wisdom and sense of justice. He is famously known for resolving a dispute between two women who both claimed to be the mother of a child. King Solomon suggested cutting the baby in half to give each woman half, but the real mother was willing to give up the child to save its life. King Solomon then awarded the baby to the real mother, demonstrating his ability to make wise and just decisions.
2. King Ashoka: King Ashoka was an ancient Indian emperor who ruled during the Maurya dynasty. He is known for promoting peace, nonviolence, and religious tolerance throughout his empire. King Ashoka implemented policies that supported his people's well-being, including building hospitals, planting trees, and establishing public works projects.
3. King Hammurabi: King Hammurabi was an ancient Babylonian king who is famous for creating the Code of Hammurabi, a set of laws that was written on a large stone pillar. The code included 282 laws that covered various aspects of daily life, including trade, agriculture, and marriage. Hammurabi's laws were designed to ensure fairness and protect the vulnerable in society.
4. King Abdulaziz: King Abdulaziz is the founder of modern Saudi Arabia.

He was known for his just governance, which included supporting education, healthcare, and infrastructure development. King Abdulaziz also implemented policies that supported women's rights and worked to modernize the country's legal system.
5. King Bhumibol Adulyadej: King Bhumibol Adulyadej was the king of Thailand for over 70 years. He was known for his dedication to improving the lives of his people, promoting sustainable development, and supporting cultural preservation. King Bhumibol Adulyadej also worked to reduce poverty and inequality in Thailand and was widely respected for his commitment to justice and fairness.

- Courage:

Courage is often associated with bravery, but it is more than just physical bravery. A courageous king is someone who is willing to take risks, stand up for what is right, and make difficult decisions. They are not afraid to speak out against injustice, even if it goes against popular opinion. A courageous king also recognizes that leadership involves vulnerability and is willing to admit their mistakes and learn from them.

A courageous king is one who is known for his bravery, determination, and fearlessness in the face of adversity. Throughout history, there have been many kings who have demonstrated courage in different ways. Here are some examples:

1. King Richard the Lionheart: Richard I of England, also known as Richard the Lionheart, was a renowned warrior and military leader. He is famous for his courage during the Crusades, particularly during the Battle of Arsuf in 1191, where he led a successful charge against the Muslim army despite being vastly outnumbered.
2. King Leonidas: Leonidas I was the king of Sparta who famously led a small force of 300 soldiers against a much larger Persian army at the Battle of Thermopylae in 480 BC. Despite the overwhelming odds,

THE QUALITIES OF A KING: WISDOM, JUSTICE, AND COURAGE

Leonidas and his men fought bravely and held off the Persians for three days before finally succumbing to the enemy.

3. King Henry V: Henry V of England is known for his victory at the Battle of Agincourt in 1415, where he led his troops to a stunning victory against a much larger French army. Despite suffering from dysentery and having fewer soldiers than the French, Henry inspired his men with a rousing speech and led them to victory through sheer determination and bravery.
4. King David: David was the second king of Israel and is known for his courage in defeating the giant Goliath with a single stone from his slingshot. He also led Israel to victory in many battles and was considered a great warrior king.
5. King Arthur: Although the legend of King Arthur is shrouded in myth and legend, he is often depicted as a courageous and chivalrous leader who fought to defend his kingdom against invaders and enemies. He is said to have led his knights into battle with honor and bravery, even in the face of overwhelming odds.

Wise, just and courageous kings have been celebrated throughout history for their ability to lead their people through difficult times, make tough decisions, and create a fair and prosperous society. Here are some examples of such kings:

1. King Solomon - Wise King of Israel: King Solomon is one of the most famous kings in the Old Testament. He is known for his wisdom, wealth, and successful reign. According to legend, Solomon was visited by God in a dream, and when asked what he wanted, he requested wisdom. God granted his request and made him the wisest man on earth. During his reign, Solomon made many wise decisions, including resolving disputes between two women claiming to be the mother of a child. He is also credited with building the first temple in Jerusalem.
2. King Ashoka - Just King of India: King Ashoka was a Mauryan emperor who ruled from 268 to 232 BCE. He is known for his transformation

from a brutal and bloodthirsty conqueror to a just and compassionate ruler. After witnessing the horrors of war, Ashoka converted to Buddhism and adopted the principles of nonviolence, tolerance, and compassion. He promoted the welfare of his subjects and built hospitals, roads, and rest houses for travelers. Ashoka is also famous for his rock edicts, which were inscriptions on rocks and pillars throughout his kingdom that proclaimed his policies and beliefs.

3. King Leonidas - Courageous King of Sparta: King Leonidas was the legendary king of Sparta who led his army against the Persians at the Battle of Thermopylae in 480 BCE. Despite being vastly outnumbered, Leonidas and his 300 Spartans fought to the death, buying time for the rest of Greece to prepare for the Persian invasion. Leonidas was known for his courage and leadership, and his sacrifice at Thermopylae became a symbol of bravery and resistance against overwhelming odds.

4. King Arthur - Wise, Just and Courageous King of Camelot: King Arthur is a legendary figure in British folklore, known for his leadership, justice, and chivalry. According to legend, Arthur was the king of Camelot and the leader of the Knights of the Round Table, a group of knights who pledged to follow a code of honor and defend the weak. Arthur is known for his wisdom, as exemplified by his decision to forgive his wife Guinevere and his best friend Lancelot for their affair, and his courage, as demonstrated by his battles against his enemies and his quest for the Holy Grail.

Together, these qualities create a powerful combination that is necessary for effective leadership. A wise, just, and courageous king is someone who is able to make decisions that benefit the greater good, while ensuring that the rights of all individuals are respected. They are able to inspire and motivate their people, creating a sense of purpose and direction. Ultimately, a king who embodies these qualities is someone who is respected, admired, and remembered long after their reign has ended.

14

The King's Advisors: Choosing the Right People, and Balancing Counsel with Personal Judgement

Choosing the right people to advise a king or any leader is crucial for the success of any endeavor. The right advisors can provide valuable insights, expertise, and guidance, helping the king make informed decisions that benefit both themselves and their subjects. However, it is equally important for a king to balance the counsel of their advisors with their own personal judgement, ensuring that they ultimately make decisions that align with their own values and goals.

When choosing advisors, a king must consider several factors. Firstly, they should look for individuals with a broad range of expertise and experience, spanning different fields and disciplines. This diversity of knowledge and perspective can help the king make well-rounded decisions that take into account all relevant factors. Additionally, the advisors should be individuals with integrity, who prioritize the well-being of the kingdom over their own personal interests. The king should also consider the advisors' track records and reputations, ensuring that they have a history of making sound decisions and providing valuable counsel.

Once advisors are chosen, the king must balance their counsel with their own personal judgement. While advisors can provide valuable insights and recommendations, ultimately the king must make decisions that align with their own values and goals. The king should consider the advice of their advisors, weighing it against their own priorities and values before making a final decision. Additionally, the king should avoid becoming overly reliant on any one advisor, seeking out the opinions of multiple advisors to gain a more comprehensive understanding of the situation at hand.

One potential pitfall that a king may encounter when balancing counsel with personal judgement is the temptation to ignore the advice of their advisors altogether. This can occur when a king becomes overly confident in their own abilities, or when they are reluctant to make a decision that conflicts with their own beliefs or desires. To avoid this, the king should remain open to feedback and criticism, taking the time to carefully consider the advice of their advisors before making a decision.

In conclusion, choosing the right advisors and balancing their counsel with personal judgement is a critical component of effective leadership. By selecting individuals with diverse expertise and experience, as well as sound track records and reputations, a king can ensure that they receive valuable guidance and recommendations. However, it is equally important for the king to maintain their own agency and decision-making power, weighing the advice of their advisors against their own priorities and values before making a final decision. By striking this balance, a king can make well-informed decisions that benefit both themselves and their subjects.

Some examples of where the wrong counsel doomed kingdoms are as follows:

- In the story of King Saul in the Bible, his trusted advisor, Ahithophel, counseled him to pursue and kill his rival, David. However, David was a beloved figure among the people, and Ahithophel's advice ultimately led to Saul's downfall and the end of his kingdom.

- In ancient Greece, the legendary King Croesus of Lydia sought the advice of the Oracle of Delphi before going to war against the Persians. The Oracle advised him that if he went to war, he would destroy a great empire. Croesus took this to mean he would emerge victorious, but in reality, his own kingdom was destroyed by the Persians.
- In medieval England, King John was advised by his counselors to impose heavy taxes on the people to fund his wars and lavish lifestyle. This caused widespread discontent among the population and eventually led to a rebellion against the king, which forced him to sign the Magna Carta and limit his powers.
- During the reign of the Mughal Emperor Aurangzeb in India, his advisors urged him to destroy the Hindu temples and shrines in the country. This led to a widespread revolt among the Hindu population and weakened the Mughal Empire's grip on the region.

Aurangzeb was known for his religious zealotry and his attempt to impose Islamic law on the Indian subcontinent. During his reign, he ordered the destruction of many Hindu temples and shrines, including the famous Kashi Vishwanath Temple in Varanasi, the Somnath Temple in Gujarat, and the Kesava Deo Temple in Mathura.

While Aurangzeb was the ultimate decision-maker in these cases, it is believed that his advisors played a significant role in urging him to undertake such actions. These advisors included Islamic scholars and clerics who believed that the destruction of Hindu temples would strengthen the Islamic faith in the region.

Some of these advisors also saw the destruction of Hindu temples as a means of demonstrating their loyalty to Aurangzeb and gaining political power and influence in his court. They argued that by destroying Hindu temples, they were upholding Islamic law and protecting the interests of the Muslim community.

However, it is important to note that not all advisors or Islamic scholars supported the destruction of Hindu temples. Some argued that such actions were against the principles of religious tolerance and that they would only serve to inflame tensions between the Muslim and Hindu communities.

In the end, the destruction of Hindu temples and shrines during Aurangzeb's reign was a highly controversial and divisive issue. While some believed that it was necessary to uphold the Islamic faith and protect the interests of the Muslim community, others saw it as a violation of religious freedom and cultural heritage.

Today, the destruction of Hindu temples and shrines is universally condemned and considered a crime against humanity. It is essential that we recognize the value of cultural diversity and religious tolerance and work towards preserving and protecting our shared cultural heritage.

- In the story of King Lear by William Shakespeare, the king's counselor, the Earl of Gloucester, advises him to banish his daughter Cordelia and split his kingdom between his other two daughters, Goneril and Regan. This advice sets off a chain of events that ultimately leads to Lear's downfall and the destruction of his kingdom.

15

Maintaining the Stability of the Kingdom: Economic Policies, Justice Systems, and Social Programs

Maintaining the stability of a kingdom requires a comprehensive approach that encompasses economic policies, justice systems, and social programs. These areas are interconnected and have a significant impact on the overall well-being of a kingdom's citizens. In this article, we will explore each of these three areas in detail and discuss how they contribute to the stability of a kingdom.

Economic Policies:

Economic policies are a crucial aspect of maintaining the stability of a kingdom. A stable and prosperous economy can provide the foundation for social programs and can reduce social inequality. There are several economic policies that can contribute to the stability of a kingdom:

1. Fiscal and Monetary Policies: The government can use fiscal and monetary policies to manage the economy. Fiscal policies involve adjusting government spending and taxation to influence economic activity. Monetary policies involve adjusting the money supply and interest rates to influence economic activity. Both policies can be used to

control inflation, stimulate economic growth, and stabilize the economy during times of recession.
2. Trade Policies: Trade policies can be used to promote economic growth and reduce poverty. The government can negotiate favorable trade agreements that promote exports and attract foreign investment. These policies can create jobs and increase economic activity.
3. Investment in Infrastructure: Investing in infrastructure such as roads, bridges, and airports can increase economic activity and create jobs. Infrastructure investments can also improve the efficiency of the economy by reducing transportation costs and improving access to markets.

Justice Systems:

Justice systems are an essential component of maintaining the stability of a kingdom. A fair and efficient justice system can promote social order and reduce crime. There are several justice system policies that can contribute to the stability of a kingdom:

1. Law Enforcement: Law enforcement agencies are responsible for maintaining public order and enforcing the law. A well-trained and well-equipped law enforcement agency can deter crime and promote social order.
2. Judicial System: A fair and efficient judicial system is essential for maintaining the rule of law. The judicial system should be independent, impartial, and transparent. It should provide fair trials and ensure that the rights of all citizens are protected.
3. Prison System: The prison system should be designed to rehabilitate offenders and prepare them for reentry into society. It should provide education, job training, and mental health services to help offenders become productive members of society.

Social Programs:
Social programs are critical to maintaining the stability of a kingdom.

Social programs can help reduce poverty, provide healthcare, and promote education. There are several social programs that can contribute to the stability of a kingdom:

1. Healthcare: Access to healthcare is essential for maintaining the health and well-being of citizens. The government can provide healthcare services or subsidize healthcare for low-income citizens.
2. Education: Education is essential for providing citizens with the skills they need to succeed in the workforce. The government can provide education services or subsidize education for low-income citizens.
3. Welfare Programs: Welfare programs can help reduce poverty and provide a safety net for citizens who are unable to work. These programs can include cash assistance, food assistance, and housing assistance.

In conclusion, maintaining the stability of a kingdom requires a comprehensive approach that encompasses economic policies, justice systems, and social programs. Each of these three areas is interconnected and has a significant impact on the overall well-being of a kingdom's citizens. By implementing effective policies in these areas, a kingdom can promote stability, reduce poverty, and improve the quality of life for its citizens.

16

Diplomacy and Warfare: Building Alliances and Preparing for Conflict

As a king, the ability to handle diplomacy and warfare is crucial to ensure the stability and security of your kingdom. Diplomacy involves building alliances, maintaining relationships with neighboring kingdoms, and negotiating treaties. On the other hand, warfare involves preparing for and engaging in battles with other kingdoms or threats to your own kingdom.

Building Alliances through Diplomacy:

To build alliances, a king needs to be able to establish positive relationships with other kingdoms. This requires diplomatic skills such as tact, negotiation, and compromise. Here are some ways in which a king can build alliances through diplomacy:

1. Send Diplomatic Missions: The king should send diplomatic missions to neighboring kingdoms to establish communication and build a rapport. This can help in establishing mutual trust and respect.
2. Exchange of Gifts: A king should exchange gifts with other kingdoms as a gesture of goodwill. These gifts can be cultural artifacts, rare commodities, or resources that are not readily available in the recipient kingdom.

3. Marriage Alliances: Marrying off a prince or princess to another kingdom can create a strong bond between two kingdoms. This can also help in avoiding conflicts in the future as the two kingdoms will be related through marriage.
4. Treaties: A king should negotiate treaties with other kingdoms to formalize their relationship. Treaties can cover issues such as trade, military support, and non-aggression pacts.

There have been many kings throughout history who have handled diplomacy with great skill and effectiveness. Here are a few examples:

1. King Solomon of Israel: King Solomon was known for his wisdom and diplomatic skills. He was able to establish alliances with neighboring countries and maintain peace during his reign.
2. Emperor Ashoka of India: Ashoka was a skilled diplomat who sent emissaries to other countries to spread Buddhism and establish peaceful relationships. He is known for his commitment to nonviolence and his efforts to promote social welfare.
3. King Louis XIV of France: Louis XIV was a master of diplomacy and was able to expand the influence of France through strategic alliances and military victories. He also used diplomacy to maintain peace in Europe during his reign.
4. King Henry VIII of England: Henry VIII was skilled at using diplomacy to further his political goals. He was able to navigate the complex political landscape of Europe and establish England as a major player on the world stage.
5. King Abdullah II of Jordan: Abdullah II is known for his diplomatic skills and his ability to maintain stability in the Middle East. He has worked to establish peaceful relationships with neighboring countries and has played a key role in regional peace talks.

Preparing for Conflict through Warfare:
Warfare is an inevitable aspect of ruling a kingdom. A king must be

prepared to defend his kingdom against external threats and also be prepared to launch military campaigns when necessary. Here are some ways in which a king can prepare for conflict through warfare:

1. Building a Strong Military: The king must build a strong military to defend his kingdom against external threats. This can be done by recruiting able-bodied men, training them in combat, and providing them with the necessary weapons and armor.
2. Fortifications: The king should build fortifications such as walls, towers, and moats to protect his kingdom from invaders. These fortifications can also be used to house the army during times of war.
3. Intelligence Gathering: A king must gather intelligence on his enemies to understand their strengths and weaknesses. This can be done by sending spies or scouts to gather information on the enemy's military, resources, and movements.
4. Planning and Strategy: A king should plan and strategize before launching a military campaign. This involves identifying the enemy's weaknesses and exploiting them, using tactics such as surprise attacks, ambushes, and flanking maneuvers.

There are many kings throughout history who are known for their skill in handling warfare. Here are a few examples:

1. Alexander the Great: Perhaps the most famous example of a king who excelled in warfare is Alexander the Great, who conquered much of the known world in the 4th century BC. He was known for his tactical brilliance, his ability to inspire his troops, and his willingness to lead from the front. He won a series of decisive battles, including the Battle of Gaugamela, which marked the beginning of his conquest of Persia.
2. Frederick the Great: Frederick II of Prussia, also known as Frederick the Great, was a military genius who is widely regarded as one of the greatest commanders in European history. He led Prussia through a series of wars, including the Seven Years' War, and transformed it into

a major European power. He was known for his strategic acumen, his ability to innovate in the face of adversity, and his willingness to take risks.

3. Julius Caesar: Julius Caesar was a Roman general and statesman who played a pivotal role in the events that led to the demise of the Roman Republic and the rise of the Roman Empire. He was known for his tactical brilliance, his ability to inspire his troops, and his willingness to take bold risks. He won a series of decisive battles, including the Battle of Alesia, which marked the end of Gallic resistance to Roman rule.

4. Saladin: Saladin was a Muslim general and statesman who is best known for his role in the Crusades. He was the first Muslim leader to unify the various factions in the Middle East and to establish a stable state. He was known for his tactical brilliance, his ability to inspire his troops, and his chivalry towards his enemies. He won a series of decisive battles, including the Battle of Hattin, which marked the beginning of the end of the Crusader states in the Middle East.

5. Sun Tzu: Sun Tzu was a Chinese general, military strategist, and philosopher who lived during the Eastern Zhou period. He is best known for his book The Art of War, which is still studied by military leaders today. He was known for his strategic acumen, his ability to outthink his opponents, and his emphasis on the importance of psychological warfare. He never fought a major battle himself, but his influence on military strategy has been enormous.

In conclusion, diplomacy and warfare are two crucial aspects of a king's rule. Building alliances through diplomacy and preparing for conflict through warfare are essential to maintaining stability and security in the kingdom. A king who is adept at diplomacy and warfare can ensure the longevity of his reign and the prosperity of his people.

Throughout history, there have been several kings who had very long reigns, some of them even lasting for more than half a century. The reasons for their longevity varied, but often included a combination of factors such as political stability, successful military campaigns, and effective leadership. Here are some of the kings with the longest reigns in history and why they were able to maintain their power for so long:

1. Louis XIV of France: 72 years, from 1643 to 1715. Louis XIV, also known as the "Sun King," was the longest-reigning monarch in European history. He became king at the age of four and ruled for over seven decades, making him a symbol of stability and continuity in France. Louis XIV centralized power in his own hands and established the French monarchy as an absolute institution. He was also a patron of the arts and architecture, commissioning many of the famous landmarks of Paris.
2. Bhumibol Adulyadej of Thailand: 70 years, from 1946 to 2016. King Bhumibol was the longest-reigning monarch in Thai history and one of the longest-reigning monarchs in the world. He ascended to the throne at the age of 18 and was widely revered as a unifying figure in Thai society. During his reign, he oversaw the modernization of Thailand's economy and society, as well as the development of its infrastructure and education system.
3. Sobhuza II of Swaziland: 82 years, from 1899 to 1982. Sobhuza II was the longest-reigning monarch in African history, having ruled over Swaziland for over eight decades. He ascended to the throne at the age of four and played a key role in the country's transition to independence from British colonial rule. He was known for his commitment to preserving Swazi culture and traditions and was widely respected by his people.
4. Franz Joseph I of Austria: 67 years, from 1848 to 1916. Franz Joseph I was the longest-reigning emperor of Austria and the last emperor of the Austro-Hungarian Empire. He ascended to the throne during a period of political turmoil in Europe and oversaw the modernization of Austria's economy and military. He also presided over a period of cultural and intellectual flourishing in Vienna, which became known as the "Golden Age" of Austrian literature and art.

5. George III of Great Britain: 59 years, from 1760 to 1820. George III was the longest-reigning monarch in British history until Queen Victoria surpassed his record in 1837. He oversaw the expansion of the British Empire and the defeat of Napoleon's armies in Europe. However, his later years were marked by mental illness, which led to a regency period during which his son, George IV, acted as king.

17

The King's Relationship with Religion and Culture: Balancing Secular and Spiritual Responsibilities

Throughout history, the relationship between religion and politics has been complex and often fraught with tension. Kings and other rulers have had to balance their secular responsibilities with their spiritual duties, navigating the sometimes conflicting demands of their political and religious roles. In this article, we will examine the historical relationship between kings, religion, and culture, and explore how monarchs have balanced their secular and spiritual responsibilities.

The Role of Religion in Monarchy

Religion has always played an important role in the lives of monarchs. In many cases, the king was seen as both a political and religious leader, responsible for maintaining order and enforcing the law, as well as for upholding the tenets of the dominant religion in the kingdom. In some cases, the king was even seen as a representative of God on earth, with a divine right to rule.

One of the earliest examples of this kind of divine monarchy can be found in ancient Egypt, where pharaohs were seen as living gods who ruled over both the physical and spiritual worlds. Similarly, in ancient China, the emperor was seen as a son of heaven, responsible for maintaining order and harmony between the heavens and the earth.

In medieval Europe, the relationship between kings and religion was similarly complex. The Catholic Church was the dominant religious institution, and the pope was seen as the spiritual leader of Christendom. Kings were expected to be devout Catholics and to uphold the teachings of the Church, but they also had to balance their spiritual responsibilities with their secular duties.

The Reformation and Beyond

The Protestant Reformation, which began in the 16th century, changed the religious landscape of Europe and had a significant impact on the relationship between kings and religion. The split between the Catholic and Protestant churches led to new tensions between monarchs and religious leaders, as kings had to navigate the competing demands of different Christian denominations.

In England, for example, Henry VIII famously broke away from the Catholic Church and created the Church of England, with himself as the head. This allowed him to divorce his wife and marry Anne Boleyn, but it also put him at odds with the pope and the Catholic Church. Subsequent monarchs had to navigate these tensions as well, with some seeking to return England to Catholicism and others embracing Protestantism.

The Enlightenment and Beyond

The Enlightenment of the 18th century brought a new focus on reason and individual rights, and challenged the traditional relationship between kings and religion. Enlightenment thinkers questioned the idea of divine right and argued for the separation of church and state. This led to the rise of secularism and the idea that government should be based on reason and science rather than religious doctrine.

Despite these changes, religion continued to play an important role in the lives of monarchs throughout the modern era. Many monarchs saw themselves as defenders of their country's religious traditions and worked to promote their particular faith. For example, Queen Victoria of England was a devout Christian and worked to promote the Church of England during her reign.

In more recent times, some monarchs have taken a more secular approach to their role. King Carl XVI Gustaf of Sweden, for example, has publicly stated that he does not see himself as a religious leader, but rather as a symbol of national unity and continuity.

Balancing Secular and Spiritual Responsibilities

Throughout history, monarchs have had to balance their secular and spiritual responsibilities, often in challenging circumstances. The tension between these two roles has led to conflict and upheaval, but it has also allowed monarchs to exercise their power in unique and meaningful ways.

Ultimately, the success of a monarch's reign depends on their ability to navigate these tensions and find a balance between their political and religious roles.

Throughout history, there have been many kings who have left a lasting legacy through their political achievements and their impact on cultural and religious traditions. Here are some examples of such kings:

1. Alexander the Great - Alexander the Great was the king of Macedonia from 336 to 323 BCE. He is known for his military conquests and his impact on Greek culture. He conquered the Persian Empire and expanded his kingdom to include parts of Egypt and India. He also founded the city of Alexandria, which became a center of learning and culture in the ancient world.
2. Julius Caesar - Julius Caesar was a Roman general and statesman who became the dictator of Rome in 44 BCE. He is known for his military conquests and his impact on Roman law and government. He reformed the calendar and introduced new laws that benefited the lower classes. He was also a patron of the arts and supported the development of Roman literature and theater.
3. Charlemagne - Charlemagne was the king of the Franks from 768 to 814

CE. He is known for his military conquests and his impact on European culture and religion. He expanded his kingdom to include much of Western Europe and was crowned the first Holy Roman Emperor in 800 CE. He supported the development of education and the arts and promoted the spread of Christianity throughout his kingdom.

4. Akbar the Great - Akbar the Great was the Mughal emperor of India from 1556 to 1605 CE. He is known for his political and religious tolerance and his promotion of the arts and culture. He abolished the jizya tax on non-Muslims and allowed people of different religions to hold high positions in government. He also supported the development of the arts and culture, including the creation of the Mughal school of painting.

5. Louis XIV - Louis XIV was the king of France from 1643 to 1715 CE. He is known for his political and cultural achievements, including the building of the Palace of Versailles and his support of the arts. He centralized power in the monarchy and promoted the idea of the divine right of kings. He also supported the development of French literature and theater, including the works of Molière and Racine.

6. Queen Elizabeth I - Queen Elizabeth I was the queen of England from 1558 to 1603 CE. She is known for her political and cultural achievements, including the defeat of the Spanish Armada and her support of the arts. She promoted the development of English literature, including the works of Shakespeare and Marlowe. She also supported the exploration and colonization of the New World.

18

The King's Legacy: Building Monuments, Writing History, and Nurturing Successors

The King's Legacy refers to the lasting impact that a monarch leaves behind through their achievements, policies, and actions during their reign. This legacy can take many forms, such as building monuments, writing history, or nurturing successors. These actions are often intended to secure the monarch's place in history and to ensure the continued prosperity and stability of the kingdom they ruled.

One way that monarchs leave a lasting legacy is by building monuments. Throughout history, monarchs have commissioned grand palaces, imposing castles, and impressive public works, such as bridges and aqueducts. These monuments serve as symbols of the monarch's power and magnificence, as well as reminders of their reign long after they are gone. The Great Pyramid of Giza in Egypt, for example, was built by Pharaoh Khufu over 4,500 years ago, and remains one of the most recognizable and enduring monuments in the world.

Another way that monarchs leave a lasting legacy is by writing history. Many monarchs throughout history have been avid patrons of the arts and humanities, and have supported the production of historical chronicles, biographies, and other works of literature that document their reign. These works serve not only to preserve the history of the monarch and their kingdom, but also to shape the way that future generations remember and understand their legacy. For example, the medieval English king, Richard III, was immortalized in the play by Shakespeare, which influenced the public perception of his reign for centuries.

Finally, monarchs can also leave a lasting legacy by nurturing successors. This involves selecting and training heirs who are capable of continuing the monarch's work and ensuring the long-term stability and prosperity of the kingdom. This can involve providing education and mentorship, as well as establishing policies and institutions that will endure beyond the monarch's own reign. For example, the Emperor Augustus of Rome famously groomed his successor, Tiberius, to ensure a smooth transition of power and the continuation of the Pax Romana.

In conclusion, the legacy of a king or queen can take many forms, but it is ultimately a testament to their impact on history and their role in shaping the course of their kingdom. Building monuments, writing history, and nurturing successors are just a few of the ways that monarchs have left their mark on the world, and these legacies continue to inspire and influence us today.

Throughout history, there have been many kings whose legacies have continued to inspire and influence us today. Here are a few examples:

1. Alexander the Great: Alexander the Great was the King of Macedonia from 336 to 323 BC. He is considered one of the greatest military commanders of all time, conquering most of the known world at the time. He is also known for spreading Greek culture throughout the regions he conquered, which had a lasting impact on the world. His tactics and military strategy are still studied today, and he is remembered as a symbol of military might and achievement.

2. Julius Caesar: Julius Caesar was a Roman statesman and general who played a critical role in the events that led to the demise of the Roman Republic and the rise of the Roman Empire. He was also a prolific writer, leaving behind works that are still studied today. He is remembered for his political savvy and military achievements, as well as his lasting impact on the Roman Empire and Western culture.
3. King Henry VIII: King Henry VIII was the King of England from 1509 to 1547. He is remembered for his six marriages and his role in the English Reformation, which saw the Church of England break away from the Roman Catholic Church. He is also known for his strong personality and political acumen, which helped him maintain power during a tumultuous time in English history. His legacy can still be seen in the Church of England and the British monarchy.
4. King Louis XIV: King Louis XIV was the King of France from 1643 to 1715. He is remembered for his role in transforming France into a modern, centralized state and for his patronage of the arts and culture. He is also known for his opulent lifestyle, which helped establish France as a cultural and economic powerhouse in Europe. His legacy can still be seen in the art, architecture, and fashion of the time, as well as in the political and cultural institutions of France.
5. King Ashoka: King Ashoka was the third emperor of the Mauryan dynasty in India, ruling from 268 to 232 BCE. He is known for his role in spreading Buddhism throughout the Indian subcontinent, as well as for his humanitarian policies and his focus on social welfare. His legacy can still be seen in the Buddhist monuments and teachings that exist in India and other parts of Asia, as well as in the focus on social welfare that exists in many modern societies.

In conclusion, the legacies of these kings continue to inspire and influence us today, shaping our political, cultural, and social institutions and leaving a lasting impact on the world.

19

Kingship in the Modern World: Evolving Concepts of Kingship in Contemporary Societies

The concept of kingship has been a prominent part of human history since ancient times. While the idea of kingship has evolved throughout history, the modern world has seen significant changes in the way that people view kingship and the role of monarchs in society.

In many modern societies, kingship is no longer viewed as an absolute monarchy where the king has complete control over the government and the people. Instead, kingship has evolved into a constitutional monarchy where the king serves as a figurehead and the government is run by elected officials.

One of the main reasons for this shift is the idea of democracy, which has become the dominant form of government in many parts of the world. In a democratic society, power is distributed among the people, and the role of the monarch is largely ceremonial. This means that the monarch's role is to represent the country, act as a symbol of national unity, and provide stability and continuity to the government.

Another factor that has contributed to the evolution of kingship in the modern world is the changing attitudes toward tradition and cultural heritage. While traditional monarchies may have been revered in the past for their historical significance and cultural symbolism, modern societies are increasingly looking for ways to modernize and adapt to changing times. As a result, many monarchies have had to adjust their roles and responsibilities to remain relevant in a rapidly changing world.

Despite these changes, however, kingship still holds an important place in many modern societies. In some countries, the monarch is seen as a unifying force that can bridge the gap between different factions and provide a sense of continuity and stability. In other countries, the monarch is seen as a symbol of national identity and pride, and serves as a reminder of the country's history and cultural heritage.

Overall, the concept of kingship in the modern world is evolving rapidly, as societies grapple with the changing roles and responsibilities of monarchs in a globalized and rapidly changing world. While the role of kings and queens may continue to change in the future, it is clear that their influence on society and culture will continue to be significant for many years to come.

In modern times, kings and monarchs have a different role and impact on the world than they did in the past. They may no longer hold absolute power, but they still have a significant influence on their respective countries and the international community. Here are some examples of modern kings and how their kingship is shaping the world:

1. King Salman bin Abdulaziz Al Saud of Saudi Arabia: King Salman has been the King of Saudi Arabia since 2015 and has been instrumental in transforming the country's economy and social policies. He has implemented reforms aimed at reducing the country's dependence on oil and promoting foreign investment. Under his reign, women have been given more rights, such as the right to drive and attend sporting events. Additionally, King Salman has played a crucial role in maintaining stability in the region and has worked to strengthen Saudi Arabia's relationships with other countries.
2. King Willem-Alexander of the Netherlands: King Willem-Alexander has been the King of the Netherlands since 2013. He has focused on

sustainability and has been involved in initiatives to reduce the country's carbon footprint. He has also promoted water management as a means of addressing climate change. King Willem-Alexander has also been an advocate for Dutch trade and has led several trade missions to different countries.

3. King Abdullah II of Jordan: King Abdullah II has been the King of Jordan since 1999 and has been a key figure in the Middle East peace process. He has worked to maintain stability in the region and has been a vocal advocate for a two-state solution to the Israeli-Palestinian conflict. King Abdullah II has also played a crucial role in promoting education and has focused on improving the quality of education in Jordan.
4. King Felipe VI of Spain: King Felipe VI has been the King of Spain since 2014 and has worked to promote economic growth and job creation in the country. He has also been an advocate for democracy and has spoken out against political extremism. King Felipe VI has also been involved in efforts to address climate change and has called for action to reduce greenhouse gas emissions.
5. King Maha Vajiralongkorn of Thailand: King Maha Vajiralongkorn has been the King of Thailand since 2016 and has focused on promoting Thai culture and traditions. He has also been involved in initiatives to improve healthcare and education in the country. Additionally, King Maha Vajiralongkorn has been an advocate for sustainable development and has worked to protect Thailand's natural resources.

These are just a few examples of modern kings and their impact on the world. While their roles and responsibilities may vary, they all have the power to shape their respective countries and the international community in significant ways.

20

Lessons from Great Kings: Case Studies of Successful Kings and their Leadership Strategies.

Throughout history, there have been many great kings who have left their mark on the world through their leadership, vision, and strategy. By studying their lives and accomplishments, we can learn valuable lessons about what it takes to be a successful leader. In this article, we will examine some of the most successful kings and their leadership strategies, and what we can learn from them.

1. King Solomon (Israel, 970-931 BC)

King Solomon is known for his wisdom, wealth, and building projects, including the construction of the first Temple in Jerusalem. Solomon's leadership style was characterized by his focus on justice and fairness, which earned him respect and loyalty from his subjects. He was also known for his diplomacy, as he established alliances with neighboring kingdoms through marriages and trade agreements. His focus on trade and commerce helped to strengthen his kingdom's economy and establish Israel as a regional power.

Lessons Learned: A leader should prioritize justice, fairness, and diplomacy, and focus on economic development and strengthening alliances.

- Julius Caesar (Rome, 100-44 BC)

Julius Caesar was a military general and politician who played a pivotal role in the transformation of the Roman Republic into the Roman Empire. Caesar's leadership style was characterized by his ability to inspire his troops and lead by example. He was also a skilled strategist, who was able to seize opportunities and turn them into victories on the battlefield. Caesar was not afraid to take risks, and his ambition and determination helped him to overcome obstacles and achieve his goals.

Lessons Learned: A leader should be able to inspire and motivate their team, be strategic and take calculated risks, and have the ambition and determination to overcome obstacles.

Julius Caesar was a Roman general and politician who played a critical role in the transformation of the Roman Republic into the Roman Empire. He was born on July 12, 100 BC, into a patrician family in Rome. His family was well-connected politically, but they were not wealthy. As a result, Caesar had to rely on his own abilities to succeed in life.

Caesar started his political career as a young man, serving as a priest and then as a prosecutor. He quickly gained a reputation for his skills as an orator and his ability to connect with people from all walks of life. In 63 BC, Caesar was elected to the position of pontifex maximus, which was the highest religious office in Rome.

During his time in office, Caesar worked to improve the lives of the Roman people. He built public works projects, such as roads and aqueducts, and he worked to reduce the influence of the nobility in Roman politics. In 60 BC, Caesar formed a political alliance with two other powerful men, Pompey and Crassus. This alliance, known as the First Triumvirate, allowed Caesar to become consul in 59 BC.

As consul, Caesar worked to pass laws that benefited the common people, including laws that provided land for the poor and reduced the power of the nobility. However, his political opponents, including the senatorial class, saw him as a threat to their power and influence. They worked to undermine him at every turn, but Caesar was able to outmaneuver them and maintain his position of power.

In 58 BC, Caesar was appointed as the governor of the province of Gaul (modern-day France). He spent the next several years campaigning against the various tribes that inhabited the region, and he was able to conquer most of them by 52 BC. His military campaigns in Gaul made him incredibly wealthy and powerful, and he was able to build a loyal army of supporters.

However, his growing power and influence made his opponents nervous, and in 49 BC, they demanded that he give up his command and return to Rome. Caesar refused, and he crossed the Rubicon River with his army, effectively declaring war on the Roman Republic. This action led to a civil war between Caesar and his opponents, which lasted for several years.

Caesar emerged victorious from the civil war, and he was named dictator for life in 44 BC. He worked to reform the government and bring stability to the Roman Empire, but his actions made him even more unpopular with his opponents. On March 15, 44 BC, a group of senators, including his close friend Brutus, assassinated him in the Roman Senate.

Julius Caesar's life offers several lessons about kingship. First and foremost, he demonstrated the importance of building a loyal and dedicated support base. Throughout his life, Caesar worked to build alliances and cultivate relationships with people from all walks of life. He was able to win the loyalty of his army and the people of Rome, which allowed him to maintain his position of power.

Additionally, Caesar showed the importance of being willing to take risks and make difficult decisions. He crossed the Rubicon River with his army, knowing that it would likely lead to a civil war, but he believed that it was necessary to protect his position of power. Similarly, he was willing to pass controversial laws and make enemies in the process, because he believed that it was the right thing to do.

Finally, Julius Caesar demonstrated the importance of being able to adapt to changing circumstances. Throughout his life, he faced numerous challenges and obstacles, but he was able to overcome them through his intelligence, cunning, and flexibility. He was able to pivot from a successful military career to a successful political career, and he was able to navigate the complex world

- Alexander the Great (Macedon, 356-323 BC)

Alexander the Great was a military commander and king who conquered a vast empire that stretched from Greece to India. Alexander's leadership style was characterized by his charisma and courage, as well as his ability to adapt to changing circumstances. He was a master of strategy and tactics, and his military campaigns were marked by his creativity and innovation. Alexander also had a deep respect for the cultures and customs of the people he conquered, which helped him to win their loyalty and support.

Lessons Learned: A leader should have charisma, courage, and adaptability, be creative and innovative in their approach, and show respect for the cultures and customs of those they lead.

Alexander III of Macedon, also known as Alexander the Great, was born in 356 BC in Pella, the capital of the ancient Macedonian kingdom. He was the son of King Philip II of Macedon and his fourth wife, Olympias. Alexander was educated by the famous Greek philosopher Aristotle, who taught him philosophy, science, and politics.

At the age of 20, Alexander became the king of Macedon after the assassination of his father. Alexander was determined to continue his father's military expansion and conquer the Persian Empire. He quickly assembled a massive army of over 30,000 men, including Macedonian soldiers and Greek mercenaries.

In 334 BC, Alexander crossed the Hellespont into Asia with his army. He won his first major battle against the Persians at Granicus and then proceeded to conquer much of Asia Minor. He went on to capture Syria and Egypt before finally reaching the Persian heartland.

Alexander's most famous battle was the Battle of Gaugamela, which took place in 331 BC. It was a decisive victory for Alexander, and it marked the end of the Persian Empire. He then went on to conquer the rest of the Persian Empire and extended his rule as far east as India.

After ten years of non-stop military campaigns, Alexander's army was exhausted, and many of his soldiers were homesick. Alexander decided to return home, but he fell ill and died in Babylon in 323 BC at the age of 32. His empire was divided among his generals, who became known as the Diadochi.

Alexander was not only a great conqueror but also a skilled leader and administrator. He implemented many reforms in the conquered territories, such as allowing local rulers to continue ruling as long as they paid tribute to him. He also encouraged the blending of Greek and Persian cultures, which led to the emergence of Hellenistic culture.

Alexander's legacy continues to inspire leaders around the world. His achievements as a conqueror are well known, but his legacy as a ruler is equally significant. He was a visionary leader who understood the importance of cultural exchange and encouraged his people to learn from other cultures. He also knew how to motivate his soldiers and inspire them to achieve great things.

One of the most important lessons that can be learned from Alexander the Great is the importance of having a clear vision and a strong sense of purpose. Alexander knew what he wanted to achieve and was determined to see his vision through to the end. He also knew the importance of building alliances and surrounding himself with talented advisors and generals.

Another important lesson from Alexander is the importance of adaptability. Alexander faced many challenges throughout his campaigns, and he was able to adapt his strategies to overcome them. He was not afraid to take risks, and he was always willing to learn from his mistakes.

Finally, Alexander was a great example of the importance of leading by example. He was not afraid to get his hands dirty and was always on the front lines of battle. His soldiers respected him because he was willing to fight alongside them and shared in their hardships.

In conclusion, Alexander the Great was a remarkable leader who accomplished great things in his short life. He was not only a brilliant military strategist but also a visionary leader who understood the importance of cultural exchange and adaptability. His legacy continues to inspire leaders around the world, and his life serves as a testament to the power of strong leadership and a clear sense of purpose.

- Charlemagne (France, 768-814 AD)

Charlemagne was a king who is credited with uniting much of Western Europe under his rule and establishing the Carolingian Empire. Charlemagne's leadership style was characterized by his commitment to education and intellectual pursuits, as well as his focus on religious reform. He was a strong and decisive leader who was able to enforce his will through the use of military force, but he also recognized the importance of diplomacy and negotiation in maintaining peace.

Lessons Learned: A leader should prioritize education and intellectual pursuits, focus on religious reform, and balance the use of force with diplomacy and negotiation.

Charlemagne, also known as Charles the Great, was a medieval ruler who was born in 742 AD and ruled the Franks from 768 AD until his death in 814 AD. He is considered one of the most important figures in European history, and his reign had a profound impact on the development of Western civilization. Charlemagne was a military leader, a religious figure, and a patron of the arts and learning. His reign was marked by significant military conquests, religious reforms, and cultural achievements.

Early Life and Rise to Power:

Charlemagne was born in 742 AD in the Frankish kingdom, which covered present-day France, Germany, Belgium, the Netherlands, and Switzerland. He was the eldest son of King Pepin the Short, who ruled the Franks from 751 AD until his death in 768 AD. Charlemagne's early years were spent at his father's court, where he received an education in the classics and military training.

When Pepin died in 768 AD, he divided his kingdom between his two sons, Charles and Carloman. However, Carloman died unexpectedly in 771 AD, leaving Charlemagne as the sole ruler of the Frankish kingdom. Charlemagne's reign was marked by a series of military campaigns aimed at expanding his kingdom and consolidating his power.

Military Campaigns:

Charlemagne was a skilled military leader who conducted a series of successful campaigns that expanded his kingdom to cover most of Western Europe. He conquered the Lombards in Italy in 774 AD, the Saxons in Germany in the 780s, and the Avars in Hungary in the 790s. He also fought against the Muslims in Spain and the Slavs in the east. His military campaigns were marked by brutality, but also by a desire to Christianize the peoples he conquered.

Religious Reforms:

Charlemagne was a devout Christian who saw himself as the defender of the faith. He was a patron of the church and worked to reform its practices. He established a system of bishops and abbots who were responsible for overseeing the spiritual life of his subjects. He also encouraged the creation of schools and the copying of religious texts, which helped spread literacy and knowledge throughout his kingdom.

Cultural Achievements:

Charlemagne's reign was marked by a flowering of learning and the arts. He encouraged the creation of manuscripts and patronized the creation of new works of art. He also established a court school that was responsible for educating his children and the sons of his nobles. This school was staffed by scholars from all over Europe and was responsible for the preservation and transmission of classical learning.

Learnings of Kingship from Charlemagne:

Charlemagne's reign provides several lessons on effective kingship. Firstly, he demonstrated the importance of military power in establishing and maintaining a kingdom. Charlemagne was a skilled military leader who understood the importance of being able to project force and defend his borders.

Secondly, Charlemagne showed the importance of religion in creating a stable and unified kingdom. He worked to Christianize the peoples he conquered and established a strong relationship with the church, which helped to legitimize his rule and ensure the support of his subjects.

Thirdly, Charlemagne demonstrated the importance of learning and culture in creating a strong and successful kingdom. He encouraged the creation of schools and the preservation of classical learning, which helped to create a common cultural identity among his subjects and ensured the long-term stability of his kingdom.

In conclusion, Charlemagne was one of the most important figures in European history, and his reign had a profound impact on the development of Western civilization. His military conquests, religious reforms, and cultural achievements provide valuable lessons on effective kingship that are still relevant today.

- King Louis XIV (France, 1638-1715 AD)

Louis XIV was a king who is known for his long and successful reign, which saw France become the dominant power in Europe. Louis XIV's leadership style was characterized by his absolute authority and his belief in the divine right of kings. He was a strong and decisive leader who was able to maintain his power through the use of propaganda and the cultivation of a powerful image. Louis XIV also understood the importance of culture and the arts in promoting his image and reinforcing his power.

Lessons Learned: A leader should have strong and decisive authority, understand the importance of image and propaganda, and prioritize culture and the arts in promoting their image.

King Louis XIV, also known as the Sun King, was born on September 5, 1638, in the Château de Saint-Germain-en-Laye, near Paris, France. He became king at the young age of 4, upon the death of his father, Louis XIII. His mother, Anne of Austria, served as regent until he came of age in 1661.

During his reign, which lasted for 72 years, Louis XIV worked tirelessly to consolidate and expand the power of the French monarchy. He established an absolute monarchy and became one of the most powerful and influential kings in European history. He was a patron of the arts, a military leader, and a shrewd politician.

One of Louis XIV's greatest achievements was the construction of the Palace of Versailles, which he used as his principal residence and a symbol of his power. He also worked to expand France's borders, engaging in numerous wars and military campaigns, which helped to make France one of the most powerful nations in Europe.

Louis XIV was known for his love of luxury, which was reflected in his lavish lifestyle and the grandeur of his court. He was also a patron of the arts, sponsoring artists such as Molière and Jean-Baptiste Lully, and he encouraged the development of French culture.

In terms of governance, Louis XIV established a centralized system of government, with himself as the ultimate authority. He appointed loyal ministers and officials to manage the affairs of state and implemented policies aimed at promoting economic growth and strengthening France's military.

Louis XIV's reign had a significant impact on the development of modern Europe, particularly in terms of the concept of the nation-state and the idea of absolute monarchy. He was a powerful and influential figure, and his reign marked the height of French power and influence in Europe.

The life of King Louis XIV provides several valuable lessons about kingship. One of the most important is the importance of strong leadership and the need for a clear vision and purpose. Louis XIV was a strong and decisive leader who knew what he wanted to achieve and worked tirelessly to achieve it.

Another important lesson from Louis XIV's life is the importance of cultivating alliances and relationships. Louis XIV was known for his ability to form strategic partnerships and alliances, which helped him to expand French power and influence.

Additionally, Louis XIV demonstrated the importance of using culture and the arts to promote national identity and pride. By sponsoring artists and writers, he helped to create a distinctly French culture, which helped to unify the nation and promote a sense of shared identity and purpose.

Overall, the life of King Louis XIV provides valuable insights into the nature of kingship and the role of strong leadership in shaping the destiny of a nation. While his reign was marked by controversy and conflict, his legacy continues to inspire and influence leaders around the world today.

www.ingramcontent.com/pod-product-compliance
Lightning Source LLC
Chambersburg PA
CBHW020453220526
45464CB00002B/969